The Hunter's Table

Best of the Best Recipes

Wild Flavors
FROM DUCK COUNTRY

The Hunter's Table

Best of the Best Recipes

Wild Flavors

FROM DUCK COUNTRY

Fruits of
Your Labor
David Maass

Fruits of Your Labor *(2004)*

David Maass   *1974, 1988, and 2004 International Artist of the Year*

An avid sportsman and ardent contributor to conservation organizations, David Maass has been actively painting game birds for more than forty years. He has designed more than thirty-five conservation stamps and prints for various states and organizations. His 1982 winning canvasback painting marks the second time that a Maass design has appeared on the Federal Duck Stamp and Print. In 1997 *U.S. Art* honored Maass with the title of Master Artist. Working mostly in oils, his artwork reveals an amazing understanding of light and a diligent study of subject matter. Three books have been published on the painting of David Maass, the most recent being *Wildfowl of North America.*

Beams Creek *(2010)*

Dennis Minor   *2000 and 2010 International Artist of the Year*

Wildlife artist Dennis Minor of Lacey's Spring, Alabama, is the Ducks Unlimited® 2010 International Artist of the Year. His painting, "Beam's Creek" earned him the top honor. "I began with DU™ many years ago as a volunteer and I remember seeing the names of guys like Jim Killen and Terry Redlin. I never thought I'd be among them. It's a real honor." Minor got the inspiration for "Beam's Creek" after hunting with this particular lab, who like all labs, managed to leave a lasting impression. "It's a typical tireless lab and the setting is someplace that hunters can relate to, no matter where they are hunting throughout the country." The flooded timber, marshy landscape with a hint of early morning fog is a setting waterfowl hunters know very well and are drawn to every fall.

The *Hunter's Table*

Wild Flavors From Duck Country

Published and Sold under License from
Ducks Unlimited, Inc.
—Leader in Wetlands Conservation.

Chapter Opener photography and four-color cover
    background © by Mike Rutherford
Wildlife art and photography courtesy of
    Ducks Unlimited,® except pages 158, 186
    © by Ralph J. McDonald
Food photography © as noted on page 192
    constitutes an extension of this copyright page

Copyright © 2010 by

Favorite Recipes® Press
an imprint of FRP, Inc.,
a wholly-owned subsidiary of
Southwestern/Great American, Inc.
P.O. Box 305142
Nashville, Tennessee 37230
1-800-358-0560

Library of Congress Control Number: 2010921053
ISBN: 978-0-87197-548-5

Manufactured in the United States of America
First Printing: 2010

Foreword

Scott Leysath

There was a time when I had decided that I much preferred hunting game to eating it. Raised on ducks that had been crammed full of an assortment of fruits and vegetables and then cooked for hours until tough and dry, I just assumed that ducks tasted like liver. My first green-winged teal, despite being wrapped in bacon, was overcooked and reminded me of a well-done old goat. It wasn't until several years later that I discovered that it was the cook, and not the game, that made the difference between inedible and truly remarkable table fare.

During the past few decades, people have dramatically changed they way they feel about both preparing and consuming food. Television cooking shows have mushroomed from a handful of notable chefs like Julia Child, Graham Kerr (The Galloping Gourmet), and Justin Wilson to entire networks devoted to cooking and watching people eat. Viewers of all ages are transfixed by "celebrity" chefs, some using obscure ingredients from faraway places and others making the ordinary appear extraordinary. There are even shows devoted to watching the hosts consume strange plants and animals, purely for the shock and entertainment value. And yet, in spite of our fascination with multicultural cuisine, there are those folks who wouldn't think of sampling grilled mallard breast with currant jelly sauce since it no doubt tastes, well, gamey. Those of us who routinely put flame to game, including the contributors to this book, understand that a properly prepared wild game feast is fine dining at its best.

This cookbook is both a testament to the evolution of wild game preparation and a tribute to the home chefs who provided hundreds of simple, yet imaginative recipes to the Ducks Unlimited® Recipe Contest. Deciding which recipes should be placed in the top five among nearly 1,500 entries was a formidable task for the DU™ Culinary Council. Oh sure, there were a few common entries. Marinating strips of game meats before wrapping with jalapeño peppers, cream cheese, and bacon is apparently not a well-kept secret, but it sure does taste great! Fortunately, our contributing home chefs ventured well beyond the obvious to create wild game recipes that are destined to take their rightful place among the best.

I applaud Ducks Unlimited® for undertaking the monumental effort required to assemble a cookbook of this caliber. They recognize that a large part of being a responsible hunter is to make the most of the game we harvest. Far too many hunters are all too eager to give away their bounty because of some misguided experience with game cookery. If your duck tastes like an old goat, don't blame the duck. You need this cookbook.

Scott Leysath

Contents

Beams Creek
Dennis Minor

NATIONAL HEADQUARTERS
One Waterfowl Way
Memphis, TN 38120-2351
(901) 758-3825 fax (901) 758-3850
www.ducks.org

Special moments from waterfowl hunts past are among my favorite memories. I suspect that many Ducks Unlimited® members share that fondness for rehashing days spent afield with close friends and family, favored shotguns, and wet retrievers. Like a fine wine, these recollections seem to grow better with age.

So, too, do I enjoy the bounty that nature provides hunters and anglers. Whether we're discussing ducks, geese, white-tailed deer, wild turkeys, quail, fish, or other wildlife, I think we can agree that all make for outstanding table fare when properly prepared.

Ducks Unlimited® members from across the nation have graciously provided the heart of this cookbook—an outstanding collection of tried-and-true recipes conceived to enhance wild game and fish. I personally can't wait to try my hand at re-creating these dishes in my kitchen. They hold great promise for extraordinary meals.

While our respective culinary skills may vary widely, those in the Ducks Unlimited® family nonetheless share a common bond. We appreciate the wildlife we pursue and recognize the importance of this organization's conservation mission. The willingness to put back more than what we take is a testament to DU™ members' commitment and belief in this noble cause. Respecting the waterfowl resource, and its needs, are at the top of our conservation agenda.

Those who acquire this book will receive not only a wealth of information regarding wild game preparation, but also the satisfaction of knowing that they are helping to perpetuate a uniquely American outdoors lifestyle. There is strength in our unity, our loyalty, and our commitment to doing the most that we can on behalf of waterfowl and wetland conservation.

Thank you for all that you do for the ducks. Bon appétit!

John R. Pope
President

The Nugent family takes our hunting lifestyle very seriously and genuinely celebrates the sacred protein from all of God's wonderful critters as a reward for a job well done. As a longtime DU™ Lifer, we are sure that a roasted mallard or woody tastes that much better for the thrill of the hunt and the hyper psyches of our quivering Labradors in a cold, wet duckblind.

God bless DU™, God bless each and every hunt, and God bless the waterfowlers' banquet!

Ted Nugent

Flyways

Flyways are denoted on waterfowl recipes submitted by Ducks Unlimited® members.

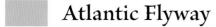 **Atlantic Flyway**

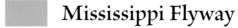 **Mississippi Flyway**

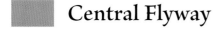 **Central Flyway**

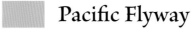 **Pacific Flyway**

Ducks Unlimited Culinary Council Chefs

Billy Joe Cross   Eileen Clarke   Lisa Freeman   Scott Leysath

Billy Joe Cross   BJC

Billy Joe has served as president of the Mississippi Flyway Council, president of the Southeastern Association of Game and Fish Directors, and executive director of the Mississippi Game and Fish Commission.

In 1966 Billy Joe became Ducks Unlimited® Regional Director, overseeing three states. During his tenure with DU,™ he subsequently served as regional supervisor, Mississippi Flyway MARSH coordinator, field operations supervisor, and director of field operations. In 1979 the Mississippi Wildlife Federation chose him as Wildlife Conservationist of the Year.

As a chef, Billy Joe has produced fifteen cooking shows for national television, including six shows sponsored by GMC®. He has also been featured on cooking shows for Mississippi ETV and WLBT Midday Mississippi in Jackson, Mississippi. In addition, Billy Joe has served as a columnist for *DU™ Magazine*. He has authored eight cookbooks, edited three, and been featured in three additional cookbooks.

Recently, Billy Joe has taught more than twenty cooking classes across the Southeast and participated in dinners to help raise millions of dollars for scholarships, athletic programs, and organizations. Billy Joe is a frequent teacher and lecturer for the Viking Culinary Institute.

Eileen Clarke   E~MC~

Eileen Clarke is the author of eight wild game cookbooks, the latest of which is *Slice of the Wild*, an all big game, bullet to fork guide to game care, cutting, and cooking. She's also in cahoots with her husband John Barsness, in writing their quarterly e-newsletter, *Rifle Loony News*. In between, she was the game care/cooking columnist for *Field & Stream* and *Successful Hunter* magazine for many years, optics columnist for *Women's Outlook*, and has contributed off-beat hunting stories to many national magazines, including *Gray's Sporting Journal, Wyoming Wildlife*, and *Montana Outdoors*, and even found time to publish a novel, *The Queen of the Legal Tender Saloon*.

Eileen has hunted all over Montana and the U.S., as well as Europe, Africa, New Zealand, and northern Canada. As one reviewer commented, "Eileen cooks things with holes in them." And, if she didn't put the hole there, her husband did. No pen-raised birds, no game farm elk; if it's in her cookbooks she's dragged it from the field—sometimes with a little help—and skinned, plucked, boned, steaked, and filleted it in her own kitchen. It's why she's sold over 200,000 cookbooks.

Eileen's books and *Rifle Loony News* are all available at www.riflesandrecipes.com.

Lisa Freeman   L~MF~

Fare Game Chef Lisa Freeman has preached the gospel of wild game and outdoor cooking from coast to coast. She provides executive chef services for NASCAR®, Inc. and is a presenting chef for Safari Club International's annual convention, with her popular "Wild Game & Wine" pairing seminar. She donates to and supports the international conservation projects of the Banovich Wildscape Foundation, is an appointed member of Ducks Unlimited® Culinary Council, and is a former columnist for *Field & Stream*. A popular wild game expert, speaker, and teacher, Lisa creates custom and interactive events that incorporate wild game and outdoor cooking in showcasing products and foods that appeal to the sporting life market.

Lisa's passion for wild game cooking shines through in her personal appearances. Her credits include culinary direction for *The Full Bloom Show* and the PBS show *Michael Chiarello's Napa* where Lisa worked with a team of chefs in culinary production. She has been featured in many national publications and hosts "Taste of the Outdoors" recipe segment within the *California Sportsman* radio show on Sacramento's KHTK 1140 AM.

Scott Leysath   S~FL~

Scott Leysath, better known as "The Sporting Chef,™" is one of America's leading authorities on the proper preparation of fish and game. He has worked in the food and beverage industry since 1978. After serving as vice-president of a thirty-three–unit restaurant chain, Leysath opened his own restaurant. There, he invited his customers to let him prepare their bagged fish and game. His catering company also provided hundreds of banquet meals for sporting groups like Ducks Unlimited®.

Leysath spent three years on HGTV's *Home Grown Cooking with Paul James*. When not hamming it up on-air with the show's host, he was Executive Chef, responsible for creating recipes for over 180 shows. His first television show, *The Sporting Chef*, has been syndicated worldwide since 2003 and his current show, *HuntFishCook*,™ airs throughout the U.S. and Canada. He makes weekly radio appearances and writes articles and recipes for national and regional outdoor publications. Chef Leysath is also the cooking editor of the *Ducks Unlimited® Magazine*.

Leysath lives in northern California, but spends a considerable amount of time across North America conducting fish and game seminars. He has a passion for hunting, fishing, and teaching others how to make the most of their catch. For more on Scott Leysath, visit www.HuntFishCook.com.

Waterfowl Winners

Appetizers • Soups & Sandwiches • Main Dishes • Grilling

First Flight

Goose Pâté

4 cups buttermilk
1/4 cup Worcestershire sauce
1/4 cup soy sauce
2 1/2 pounds deboned goose or duck
1/2 cup Worcestershire sauce
1/2 cup soy sauce
1 red onion, chopped
2 cups chopped celery
2 cups pickle relish
5 to 7 hard-cooked eggs, sliced
1 1/2 to 2 cups mayonnaise
1 tablespoon pepper
1/2 teaspoon garlic salt
1 1/2 tablespoons ranch salad dressing mix
1 teaspoon ham or steak seasoning
Salt or seasoned salt to taste
1 hard-cooked egg, sliced
Chopped fresh parsley

Serves 20

Mix the buttermilk, 1/4 cup Worcestershire sauce and 1/4 cup soy sauce in a large bowl and add the goose. Marinate, covered, in the refrigerator overnight; drain. Cover the goose with water in a large saucepan. Stir in 1/2 cup Worcestershire sauce and 1/2 cup soy sauce. Bring to a boil and boil for 40 minutes or until cooked through. Drain, reserving 1/2 cup liquid.

Grind the warm goose into a bowl. Stir in 1/4 cup of the reserved cooking liquid, the onion, celery, relish and 5 to 7 eggs. Combine the mayonnaise, pepper, garlic salt, salad dressing mix and ham seasoning in a bowl and mix well. Add to the goose mixture and toss to mix. Stir in 1/4 cup reserved cooking liquid if mixture seems too dry. Season with salt.

Spoon into a serving bowl and garnish with 1 sliced egg and parsley. Serve with crackers, pita chips or cocktail bread.

Note: This also freezes well. You may use any goose or duck pieces or leftover trim for this pâté. This tastes so much like beef pâté our friends can't believe it's wild game.

 Mark Bosh

Duck Pâté

2 pounds duck breasts
2 tablespoons baking soda
1/2 yellow onion
2 garlic cloves, chopped
4 ounces sweet pickle relish
4 ounces hot and sweet pickle chips
1 cup mayonnaise-type salad dressing
1 tablespoon Louisiana hot sauce
1 teaspoon each salt, pepper and ground cumin

Serves 16

Cut the duck breasts into 1-inch cubes. Bring 8 cups water to a boil in a saucepan. Add the baking soda and stir until dissolved. Add the duck. Boil until cooked through; drain.

Grind the warm duck, onion, garlic, pickle relish and pickle chips into a bowl. Stir in the salad dressing, hot sauce, salt, pepper and cumin. Chill until cold. Serve with crackers.

 Greg Meier

Duck Fingers

1 1/2 cups baking mix
1 cup instant potato flakes
1 tablespoon lemon pepper
1 teaspoon garlic powder
1/2 teaspoon onion powder
1/4 teaspoon coarsely ground
black pepper
1 egg
1 cup beer
4 boneless skinless duck or goose
breasts, cut into 1-inch strips
Vegetable oil for deep-frying

Serves 12

Mix the baking mix, potato flakes, lemon pepper, garlic powder, onion powder and black pepper in a bowl. Add the egg and beer and mix well. Rinse the duck strips and pat dry. Heat oil to 360 degrees in a deep fryer. Dip the duck strips, one at a time, into the batter, allowing any excess to drain. Fry in the hot oil for 4 to 6 minutes or until golden brown and cooked through. Serve plain or with dipping sauces.

Note: Blue cheese or ranch salad dressings or salsa make good dipping sauces.

 Adam Kats

Teal Tenders

4 (1-pound) boneless skinless
teal breasts
1 sprig of rosemary, chopped
1/2 teaspoon salt
1 teaspoon lemon pepper
1 1/2 teaspoons garlic powder
1 cup fine bread crumbs
1/2 cup whole milk
2 tablespoons bourbon
Vegetable oil for deep-frying

Serves 12

Brine the teal in your favorite brining solution in a bowl in the refrigerator for 4 hours. Drain and slice the teal into 1/2-inch strips lengthwise. Mix the rosemary, salt, lemon pepper, garlic powder and bread crumbs in a shallow dish. Mix the milk and bourbon in a small bowl. Dip the teal strips in the milk and coat in the bread crumbs, repeating the process if a thicker coating is desired. Heat oil in a deep fryer. Fry 4 to 6 strips at a time in a wire mesh basket in the deep fryer for 2 to 4 minutes or until golden brown and cooked through. Remove to paper towels to drain. You may also cook these in hot oil in a skillet on the stovetop.

Note: This recipe was created for the time it takes to deep-fry a turkey and we needed something to accompany our libations. If deep-frying a turkey, you can use the same oil.

 Nicholas Walker

DUCK SAMPLER

2 tablespoons extra-virgin olive oil
1 (8-ounce) duck breast
Salt and freshly ground pepper to taste
Platter of diced buffalo mozzarella
cheese, assorted olives, herb goat
cheese, crackers and bread

4 servings

Heat the olive oil in a sauté pan over medium-high heat. Season the duck breast with salt and pepper. Place duck breast in the pan and sear until browning begins. Turn over and sear on the other side. Cooking process should not take longer than 5 minutes. Do not overcook. You definitely want it between rare to medium-rare. Slice and serve with the cheese and olive platter.

LMF

Duck is one of my favorites when it comes to cooking game. If you are having guests over and want to provide something tasty to snack on, seared duck breast and some great cheeses with cured olives are a perfect beginning. The trick is how you cook the duck!! Also great to pack along for snacks when out for a day of hiking, etc.

DUCK SPRING ROLLS

1 cup shredded carrots
1 cup sliced shiitake mushrooms
1 small head bok choy or napa
cabbage, shredded
Peanut oil for frying
1 pound cooked duck breast,
chopped or pulled
1/3 cup soy sauce
24 spring roll wrappers
Hoisin sauce

Serves 24

Sauté the carrots, mushrooms and cabbage in a small amount of peanut oil in a skillet until tender. Add the duck and soy sauce and sauté for 1 minute. Remove from the heat and let cool slightly. Lay 1 spring roll wrapper with a point at the bottom on a work surface. Brush the edges with water. Spoon 1/4 cup of the filling into the bottom corner of the wrapper. Fold the bottom point over the filling and fold in the sides. Roll up snugly. Press lightly to seal. Repeat with the remaining wrappers and filling. Heat a shallow layer of peanut oil in a deep skillet over medium heat. Add the spring rolls and cook for 2 minutes or until golden brown, turning as needed. Remove to paper towels to drain. Serve with hoisin sauce.

 Jason Lemmink

TERIYAKI GOOSE SPRING ROLLS

2 snow goose breasts, or 1 Canada
goose breast
1/2 cup soy sauce
1/4 cup packed brown sugar
1 teaspoon granulated garlic
1 teaspoon ginger
1/2 teaspoon salt
1/2 teaspoon pepper
1 tablespoon vegetable oil
1 (14-ounce) can bean sprouts,
drained and chopped
1/2 cup shredded green cabbage
1/2 cup finely chopped green onions,
white and green parts
1/2 cup chopped bamboo shoots
1/2 green bell pepper, finely chopped
10 spring roll wrappers
1 egg, beaten
1 to 2 cups vegetable oil
2 cups shredded red cabbage
1 tablespoon toasted sesame seeds

Serves 10

Place the goose in a sealable plastic bag. Combine the soy sauce, brown sugar, garlic, ginger, salt and pepper in a bowl and mix well. Remove and reserve 2 tablespoons of the marinade. Pour the remaining marinade over the goose. Seal the bag tightly and turn to coat. Marinate in the refrigerator for 8 hours to overnight, turning once or twice. Remove the goose and discard the marinade.

Heat 1 tablespoon oil in a skillet. Add the goose and fry until cooked through. Remove the goose to a work surface and let cool. Shred the goose meat, discarding the skin and bones. Mix the goose, bean sprouts, green cabbage, green onions, bamboo shoots and bell pepper in a bowl. Add 2 tablespoons reserved marinade and mix well.

Lay the spring rolls on a work surface and brush the edges with the egg. Fill each spring roll wrapper with about 3 heaping tablespoons of the goose mixture and roll up using the package directions. Press lightly to seal.

Heat 1 to 2 cups oil to 350 degrees in a deep skillet. Fry the spring rolls, 4 or 5 at a time, for 4 to 6 minutes or until golden brown, turning once. Remove to paper towels to drain.

Spread the red cabbage over a serving plate. Cut each spring roll in half diagonally and arrange over the red cabbage. Sprinkle with the sesame seeds and serve.

 Ralph Nestor

Ducks Unlimited® is the *only* waterfowl conservation organization working with both public and private landowners in Arkansas to restore, create, and enhance habitat for wintering waterfowl.

Duck Rangoon Won Tons with Sweet-and-Sour Sauce

For the Sweet-and-Sour Sauce
6 tablespoons pineapple juice
2 tablespoons brown sugar
2 tablespoons hoisin sauce
1 tablespoon rice wine vinegar
2 teaspoons cornstarch

For the Won Tons
8 ounces diced or ground duck meat
8 ounces cream cheese, softened
1 teaspoon prepared
creamy horseradish
2 green onions, chopped
1 (1-pound) package
won ton wrappers
Peanut or canola oil for fryer

Makes about 60

The Sauce: In a small bowl, combine the pineapple juice, brown sugar, hoisin sauce, vinegar and cornstarch. Stir to dissolve the cornstarch.

Microwave on High (700 watts) for about 1 minute, or until the sauce starts to boil and thicken a bit. Set aside. (Sauce is best at room temperature.)

The Won Tons: In a food processor, combine the duck meat, cream cheese and horseradish. Process just until the mixture is chopped, pulsing off and on 1 or 2 seconds at a time, 4 or 5 times. When done, add the chopped green onions and stir by hand.

Place the won ton wrappers on a cutting board 4 or 5 at a time. Place 1 teaspoon of filling in the center of each. Lightly moisten the edges of the wrappers. Then fold in half, corner to corner, so you have triangles. Fold the long ends together, moisten the corners and press to seal. Repeat until you're done.

Preheat the oil in a fryer. (Temperature should be around 375 degrees for best results.) Cook the won tons in batches, without crowding, until crisp and golden brown, about 2 minutes, turning once to brown evenly. Drain on paper towels as you proceed with the next batch.

To serve, dip in sweet-and-sour sauce.

EMC

I love finger food, and this is one of my favorites for parties. You can either fill and fold the won tons and keep them refrigerated until you're ready to cook and eat them, or just go whole hog and hold the finished won tons in a 250-degree oven for up to an hour.

KENTUCKY FRIED DUCK

4 boneless duck breasts, cut into
1-inch strips
1 cup soy sauce
Dash of Worcestershire sauce
1 shot of high-quality
Kentucky bourbon
1 teaspoon garlic powder
1 teaspoon salt
1 teaspoon pepper
1 teaspoon paprika
Dash of cinnamon
3 cups self-rising flour
2 cups olive oil

Serves 12

Place the duck in a sealable plastic bag. Mix the soy sauce, Worcestershire sauce, bourbon, garlic powder, salt, pepper, paprika and cinnamon in a bowl and pour over the duck. Seal tightly and turn to coat. Marinate in the refrigerator for at least 1 hour. Remove the duck and discard the marinade.

Place the flour in a sealable plastic bag. Add the duck, a few pieces at a time, and toss to coat. Heat the olive oil to 350 degrees in a large heavy skillet. Add the duck and fry for 3 minutes per side or until cooked through. Remove to paper towels to drain. Let stand for 2 minutes before serving.

 Bryan Slaughter

SPICY DUCK FRIES

1 pound boneless duck breasts,
cut into strips
2 eggs
1 (5-ounce) can evaporated milk
1 tablespoon baking powder
2 tablespoons vinegar
1 cup all-purpose flour
Creole seasoning
Peanut oil for deep-frying

Serves 6 to 8

Place the duck in a sealable plastic bag. Whisk the eggs, evaporated milk, baking powder and vinegar in a bowl and pour over the duck. Seal tightly and turn to coat. Marinate in the refrigerator for at least 1 hour. Remove the duck and discard the marinade.

Place the flour in a shallow dish and season with Creole seasoning. Dip the duck in the flour mixture to coat. Heat peanut oil to 380 degrees in a deep heavy skillet. Add the duck and fry until cooked through. Remove to paper towels to drain.

 Zack Thompson

GOOSE IN PUFF PASTRY

2 cups chopped goose
1/4 cup (1 ounce) chopped Brie cheese or Monterey Jack cheese
1/4 cup chopped morel or other mushroom
1/8 teaspoon chopped chives
Pinch of thyme
Pinch of salt
1/8 teaspoon pepper
1 (16-ounce) package puff pastry, thawed
1 egg, beaten

Makes about 16

Soak the goose in cold water in a bowl for at least 45 minutes, changing the water occasionally; drain. Combine the goose, cheese, mushroom, chives, thyme, salt and pepper in a food processor and process just until chopped.

Roll out each sheet of pastry on a floured surface to one-half the original thickness. Cut into sixteen 4×4-inch squares. Drain the goose mixture, if needed. Spread about 2 tablespoons of the goose mixture over each pastry square.

Roll out the remaining sheet of pastry to one-half the original thickness. Cut into sixteen 4×4-inch squares. Cover each filled pastry square with a plain pasty square and press the edges with a fork to seal. Arrange the filled pastries on a nonstick baking sheet and brush with the egg.

Bake at 350 degrees for 20 to 25 minutes or until golden brown. Remove to a wire rack and cool for 15 minutes before serving.

 David Thompson

There are many substitutions that can be made with this recipe. Try Parmesan cheese and basil instead of Brie and thyme and offer marinara as a dipping sauce. Feel free to play around with the ingredients. This appetizer goes well with a riesling or chardonnay.

The United States has lost more than half of its original wetlands and continues to lose more than 80,000 acres of the wetlands most important to wildlife each year.

TOSTADITAS

2 tablespoons oil
4 ounces ground duck/goose
1/4 cup minced onion
1 tablespoon chopped green pepper
1 garlic clove, minced
3/8 teaspoon chili powder
1/4 teaspoon salt
1/4 teaspoon ground black pepper
2 tablespoons sour cream
1 cup chopped ripe tomatoes
1/2 cup chopped yellow onion
1/2 teaspoon (canned) chopped
jalapeño chile
2 teaspoons chopped fresh cilantro
Oil for deep-frying
6 (5- to 6-inch) corn tortillas
2 ounces shredded Cheddar cheese

Makes about 40 bite-size snacks

In a large skillet, heat 2 tablespoons oil over medium heat and brown the ground meats. Add 1/4 cup minced onion, green pepper and garlic and sauté until softened. Add the chili powder, salt and pepper. Turn the heat off and add the sour cream. Cover and set this aside.

Combine the tomatoes, 1/2 cup chopped onion, jalapeño chile and cilantro. Mix well.

Preheat oil in a deep fryer. Cut each tortilla into 8 wedges. When the oil is hot, dip each segment into the hot oil and fry until crisp, about 3 or 4 minutes each. Drain on paper towels.

Spread some of the meat mixture on the tortilla chips, then a bit of the cheese, and top with the salsa.

EMC

The best kind of finger food for the holidays, or for a quiet afternoon once the season is over. But make lots: These mini-tacos will disappear like Canada geese do when you finally get a day off.

Duck Blind Jerky

4 to 5 pounds boneless skinless
wild duck or goose breast
1¹/₂ cups soy sauce
1¹/₂ cups teriyaki marinade
2 tablespoons Tabasco sauce
3 tablespoons Worcestershire sauce
2 teaspoons onion powder
2 teaspoons garlic salt
2 teaspoons black pepper
¹/₄ teaspoon cayenne pepper
1¹/₂ teaspoons liquid smoke
¹/₄ teaspoon chili powder
1 tablespoon minced garlic
1 tablespoon barbecue sauce
¹/₄ cup packed brown sugar
1¹/₂ cups water
³/₄ cup beer
Black pepper or crushed red pepper
(optional)

Makes 1 pound

Place the duck in the freezer until partially frozen for easier cutting. Slice the duck into ¹/₄-inch strips. Combine the soy sauce, teriyaki marinade, Tabasco sauce, Worcestershire sauce, onion powder, garlic salt, 2 teaspoons black pepper, the cayenne pepper, liquid smoke, chili powder, garlic, barbecue sauce, brown sugar, water and beer in a large stainless steel bowl and stir until the sugar is dissolved. Stir in the duck, being certain all of the duck is submerged in the liquid. Marinate in the refrigerator for 24 hours or longer. Remove the duck and discard the marinade.

Arrange the duck in a single layer on butcher paper. Sprinkle with black or red pepper and let stand for 15 minutes. Arrange the meat in a food dehydrator or smoker and dry for 8 hours, using the manufacturer's directions. If smoking, use only 1 pan of chips. Enjoy immediately or freeze for up to 3 months in sealable plastic freezer bags.

 Jason Graham

Wood Duck Salad

1 cup balsamic vinegar
2 boneless wood duck breasts
1 package fresh field greens
8 ounces pine nuts, toasted
8 ounces crumbled blue cheese
Additional balsamic vinegar

Serves 4

Cook 1 cup vinegar in a small saucepan over medium-high until reduced to a thick syrup. Arrange the duck in a baking dish and brush with the reduced vinegar. Bake at 350 degrees until a meat thermometer inserted into the thickest portion registers 140 degrees.

Remove the duck to a cutting board and thinly slice. Arrange the field greens on chilled salad plates. Top with the pine nuts and cheese. Arrange the sliced duck over the cheese and drizzle with additional vinegar. Serve immediately.

 Brad Barricklow

SMOKED DUCK SALAD

2 cups smoked duck, shredded
1/2 cup celery, diced
1/2 cup red onion, diced
1/3 cup carrots, peeled and diced
1/2 cup marinated artichoke
hearts, quartered
1/4 cup black olives, chopped
1/4 cup pecan pieces,
roasted and chopped
1/2 teaspoon salt
1/4 teaspoon pepper
1/3 cup white wine vinegar
1 teaspoon lemon juice
1 garlic clove, minced
1 teaspoon Dijon mustard
Pinch of granulated sugar
2 tablespoons fresh basil, minced
1/2 cup olive oil
4 handfuls romaine lettuce, chopped
2 tomatoes, quartered

Serves 4

In a medium bowl, combine smoked duck with the next 8 ingredients and toss.

In another bowl, whisk together vinegar and the next 5 ingredients. While whisking, add oil in a thin stream until emulsified. Add dressing to salad mixture, reserving a few teaspoons to drizzle over lettuce. Toss to coat salad mixture.

Mound lettuce on plates. Mound salad over lettuce. Garnish with tomatoes and drizzle reserved dressing over lettuce and tomato.

SFL

Oklahomans know more than most about how to smoke meats. I often use smoked duck for sandwiches, salads, and great-tasting soups. Here's a smoked duck salad I "borrowed" from a good friend from Tulsa. Thanks, Paul! If you want to save some time, just toss the salad ingredients with your favorite Italian dressing.

DUCK SOUP

Duck Stock

8 to 10 duck carcasses, more bodies
equals more flavor
2 large carrots, chopped
3 ribs celery, chopped
1 yellow onion, chopped
6 garlic cloves
Cheap red wine
1 tablespoon black peppercorns
Bouquet garni (a bunch of herbs tied
together with string)

Soup

1^1/$_2$ cups carrots, peeled and diced
1^1/$_2$ cups celery, diced
1 cup yellow onion, peeled and diced
2 cups cooked smoked sausage, diced
3 cups small mushrooms, whole
2 cups cooked barley

Serves 6 to 8

The Stock: Place duck carcasses and next 4 ingredients in a large roasting pan. Spray contents with pan spray. Place in a preheated 400-degree oven for 1^1/$_2$ hours, turning contents every 20 minutes until evenly browned.

Add contents of the roasting pan to a large stockpot. Pour some wine into the roasting pan to loosen any bits stuck to the pan. Pour wine and loosened bits into the stockpot. Pour 2 cups red wine into stockpot and just enough water to cover contents of the pot. Add peppercorns and bouquet garni. Simmer, uncovered, over low heat for 6 to 8 hours, making sure that you keep just enough liquid in the pot to cover contents.

Cool to room temperature and pour contents through a colander covered with cheesecloth into a large bowl. Discard solids in colander. Transfer liquid (stock) to a medium stockpot.

The Soup: Add soup contents to stock and simmer over medium heat just until carrots are soft. Serve in bowls topped with cheese and/or croutons.

SFL

You can watch a video clip of this recipe at www.My OutdoorTV.com!

Gather up a bunch of duck carcasses, legs, and thighs and make a batch of delicious Duck Soup. This is a good way to make use of duck parts that we usually discard. You can also get rid of the root ends and trimmed pieces of carrots, celery, and onions (even onion skins are OK!). "Cheap red wine" should be dry, unflavored, and unsweetened. A big jug of burgundy works fine.

SMOKY DUCK SOUP

2 smoked duck carcasses,
with some meat on
1 (16-ounce) can whole kernel
corn, drained
1 1/2 teaspoons chopped (canned)
jalapeño chiles
1/2 to 1 whole fresh jalapeño chile
(about 3 inches in length), sliced

Serves 2 to 4

In a large pot, break up the birds into 3 or 4 pieces and cover with cold water. Bring to a boil, then set on the back burner, on simmer, with the cover slightly ajar. Simmer this way, allowing the steam to escape, for 4 to 5 hours until you have a potent broth.

Remove the duck pieces from the stockpot and let cool enough to handle. Then pluck the meat from the bones (removing most of the skin) and return the meat to the broth. Add the corn and the canned jalapeños and let the soup come back to a gentle boil. Add the sliced fresh jalapeño at the table, and serve with hot cornbread and chilled Mexican beer.

EMC

*J*ohn Zent is an avid duck hunter, as well as editor of American Hunter *magazine. This soup, made from a broth of smoked birds, is proof that he's also an avid and adventurous cook. As with all recipes, adapt this to the smoked ducks you have on hand: John recommends ten to twelve ducks. But when I first went to make it, I had only two smoked ducks in the fridge. (Each had been high-graded, but lots of meat was left.) So for starters, here's a two-duck version of John's soup that can be multiplied to fit your own resources. And, of course, if you want a really meaty soup, save the breast meat of one of those smoked ducks to sweeten the pot.*

WILD RICE SOUP

6 tablespoons butter
1 tablespoon chopped onion
1/2 cup all-purpose flour
3 cups chicken broth
3 cups cooked wild rice
2 cups cooked duck leg meat
1/3 cup finely chopped ham
1/2 cup grated carrots
3 tablespoons slivered almonds
Salt and pepper to taste
1 cup half-and-half

Serves 6 to 8

Melt the butter in a saucepan. Add the onion and sauté until tender. Add the flour and cook for a few minutes, stirring constantly. Add the broth gradually, stirring constantly. Stir in the rice, duck, ham, carrots, almonds, salt and pepper. Simmer for 5 minutes. Stir in the half-and-half and cook just until heated through.

Note: Some grocery stores carry canned rice wild, which saves having to cook the rice.

 Dudley Friskopp

GOOSE CHILI VERDE

1 goose
1 pound hot Italian sausage, chorizo or andouille, chopped or crumbled
1 onion, chopped
4 garlic cloves, chopped
2 cups beef broth
12 to 14 ounces canned chopped green chiles, drained
1 chipotle chile, chopped (optional)
2 bay leaves
1 tablespoon ancho chile powder
Salt to taste
1 tablespoon all-purpose flour (optional)

Serves 4

Remove the skin from the goose and bone the breast. Cut the breast meat into cubes. Leave the meat on the leg and thigh bones. Brown the sausage in a heavy saucepan, stirring until cooked through. Remove the sausage with a slotted spoon to a bowl.

Add the goose to the drippings in the saucepan and brown on all sides. Add the onion and sauté until tender. Add the garlic and sauté for 1 minute. Add the broth and cook, stirring constantly and scraping up any browned bits from the bottom of the pan. Stir in the sausage, green chiles, chipotle chile, bay leaves, chile powder and salt. Simmer, covered, for 1 1/2 hours or until the goose meat is tender. Simmer, uncovered, until the chili thickens slightly.

You may remove a small amount of chili to a bowl and stir in the flour. Add the mixture back to the chili and cook until thickened, stirring frequently. Remove and discard the bay leaves before serving.

 R. D. Farris

DUCK CHILI

2 tablespoons vegetable oil
1 pound ground beef
1 to 1¹/2 pounds cubed duck breast
1 onion, chopped
2 garlic cloves, minced
4 jalapeño chiles, chopped
2 bay leaves
1 teaspoon salt
2 (14-ounce) cans diced tomatoes
4 potatoes, peeled and cut into
¹/2-inch cubes
2 (15-ounce) cans dark red
kidney beans
1 (15-ounce) can black beans
1 (15-ounce) can pinto beans

Serves 8

Heat the oil in a 6-quart stockpot. Stir in the ground beef, duck, onion and garlic. Cook for 10 to 15 minutes or until the ground beef is crumbly, stirring frequently; drain.

Stir in the jalapeño chiles, bay leaves, salt, tomatoes and potatoes. Bring to a boil. Reduce the heat and simmer for 30 minutes. Stir in the kidney beans, black beans and pinto beans and simmer for 15 minutes. Remove and discard the bay leaves.

Serve garnished with shredded Cheddar cheese and sliced green onions.

 Craig Heyer

BLACK BEAN GOOSE CHILI

8 ounces bacon
2 tablespoons vegetable oil
2 large onions, chopped
8 garlic cloves, minced
3 pounds boneless goose
breast, chopped
¹/3 cup unseasoned chili powder
3 tablespoons ground cumin
1¹/2 tablespoons oregano
³/4 teaspoon cayenne pepper,
or to taste
6 cups beef broth
Salt and black pepper to taste
2 (16-ounce) cans black
beans, drained

Serves 6 to 8

Cook the bacon in the oil in a skillet until crisp. Remove the bacon with tongs to paper towels to drain; crumble. Remove half the bacon drippings to a large heavy saucepan.

Sauté the onions and garlic in the remaining drippings in the skillet over medium heat until tender. Brown the goose in the drippings in the saucepan. Stir in the onion mixture, chili powder, cumin, oregano and cayenne pepper. Sauté over high heat for 5 minutes. Stir in the broth and bacon and bring to a boil. Reduce the heat and simmer for 1¹/2 hours. Season with salt and black pepper. Stir in the beans and simmer for 30 minutes.

Serve topped with shredded cheese or sour cream.

 Tom Ford

DUCK GUMBO

6 to 8 large ducks, split in half
Chicken or beef broth
6 tablespoons Old Bay Seasoning
2 tablespoons garlic powder
1 tablespoon oregano
1 tablespoon salt
3 tablespoons filé powder
5 bay leaves
4 large yellow onions,
coarsely chopped
4 red bell peppers, coarsely chopped
1 cup olive oil
1 1/2 cups all-purpose flour
20 ounces frozen cut okra, thawed
2 pounds shelled large shrimp
1 1/2 pounds andouille, kielbasa or
any smoked sausage, sliced

Makes about 2 gallons

Place duck in a large pot, cover with water, bring to a boil and simmer for 5 to 6 hours or until meat can be easily removed.

Pull meat from bone, roughly chop and set aside. Strain liquid into another large pot over medium heat, adding additional chicken or beef broth to make 3 quarts of liquid. Add Old Bay Seasoning and the next 7 ingredients. Simmer until onions are translucent.

While simmering, heat oil in a heavy skillet over medium-high heat. Slowly whisk in flour, stirring constantly until mixture (roux) is chocolate brown, but not burnt. Remove from heat and allow to cool completely before stirring roux into pot. Add reserved duck, okra, shrimp and sausage and stir. Simmer for 10 minutes. Remove bay leaves before serving.

SFL

WILD DUCK ANDOUILLE GUMBO

1/2 teaspoon salt
1/2 teaspoon black pepper
1/2 teaspoon cayenne pepper
1/2 teaspoon white pepper
1/2 teaspoon paprika
1/2 teaspoon onion powder
1/2 teaspoon garlic powder
2 cups chopped wild duck
1 1/4 cups all-purpose flour
1 1/4 cups vegetable oil
1 cup chopped onion
1 cup chopped green bell pepper
3/4 cup chopped celery
8 cups chicken stock
1 1/2 cups chopped andouille
1 teaspoon minced garlic
3/4 cup sliced okra
Salt and black pepper to taste
Hot red pepper sauce to taste
Hot cooked rice

Serves 6

Mix the salt, black pepper, cayenne pepper, white pepper, paprika, onion powder and garlic powder in a bowl and mix well. Sprinkle half of the seasoning mixture over the duck in a bowl and toss to coat. Let stand for 30 minutes. Mix the remaining seasoning and half the flour in a bowl. Add to the duck and toss to coat.

Heat 1/4 cup of the oil in a heavy saucepan until very hot. Add the duck and fry until golden brown and cooked through. Remove the duck to paper towels to drain.

Add the remaining 1 cup oil to the saucepan and heat over high heat, stirring constantly and scraping up any browned bits from the bottom of the pan. Whisk in the remaining flour gradually. Cook for 3 to 4 minutes or until the mixture is very dark brown, whisking constantly. Remove from the heat and stir in the onion, bell pepper and celery.

Cook over medium heat until the vegetables are tender, stirring constantly. Stir in the stock gradually. Bring to a boil. Reduce the heat. Stir in the sausage, garlic, okra and duck. Simmer for 15 to 25 minutes or until thickened, stirring frequently. Season with salt, black pepper and hot sauce. Serve over rice.

 Tom Balk

Across the country, Ducks Unlimited® members attend
more than 4,500 fund-raising events each year.

DUCK GUMBO

1 cup vegetable oil
1 cup flour
1 rib celery, finely chopped
6 garlic cloves, chopped
8 onions, finely chopped
3 bell peppers, chopped
12 cups (3 quarts) water or stock
6 to 8 ducks, cooked, skinned and deboned
1 (10-ounce) can diced tomatoes and green chiles
2 ounces Kitchen Bouquet
1/2 teaspoon thyme
1/2 teaspoon ground oregano
1 bay leaf
1 (10-ounce) package frozen okra
2 tablespoons salt
1 tablespoon pepper

Serves 8 to 10

Heat oil in a large flat-bottom pan. Add the flour and cook until chocolate brown, stirring constantly. Add the celery, garlic, onions and bell peppers. Cook until vegetables are tender, stirring often. Add the water, duck, tomatoes, Kitchen Bouquet, thyme, oregano and bay leaf and simmer over very low heat for 1 hour. Do not allow mixture to boil. Add the okra, salt and pepper after 30 minutes. Remove bay leaf before serving.

Variation: For seafood gumbo, add 5 pounds of peeled shrimp and 6 small cans of crab claw meat 20 minutes before end of cooking period.

Notes: To get the best-tasting duck meat for this recipe, boil ducks in water to cover with a bay leaf.

If you achieve a dark brown roux for this recipe, you may eliminate the Kitchen Bouquet, which is primarily used to give foods an attractive brown color.

BJC

Ducks Unlimited®, Inc. is recognized as the world's largest and most effective waterfowl and wetlands conservation organization.

GOOSE GUMBO

1 cup all-purpose flour
1 cup vegetable oil
1 pound andouille, cut into
1/2-inch slices
1 cup chopped onion
1/2 cup chopped green bell pepper
2 garlic cloves, minced
1 goose breast, cooked, deboned and
cut into 1-inch chunks
1 package frozen cut okra
1/2 cup chopped celery
2 bay leaves
1 1/2 teaspoons Cajun seasoning
1 teaspoon salt
1/2 teaspoon thyme
1/4 teaspoon pepper
1 tablespoon filé powder
Dash of hot red pepper sauce
1 tablespoon Worcestershire sauce
8 cups water
4 cups hot cooked rice
3/4 cup sliced green onions

Serves 4

Whisk the flour into the oil in a skillet. Cook the roux over medium-high heat to a dark brown color, whisking constantly. Remove from the heat.

Sauté the sausage, onion, bell pepper and garlic in a heavy saucepan until the sausage is browned and the vegetables are tender; drain. Stir in the roux, goose, okra, celery, bay leaves, Cajun seasoning, salt, thyme, pepper, filé powder, hot sauce, Worcestershire sauce and water. Simmer, covered, for 1 to 1 1/2 hours, stirring occasionally.

Remove and discard the bay leaves. Divide the rice among four serving bowls and top with the gumbo. Sprinkle with the green onions and serve.

 H. James Schierstein

CAROLINA DUCK STEW

1 pound bulk pork sausage
8 ounces smoked sausage, chopped
4 onions, chopped
4 cups water
2 ducks, quartered
Salt and pepper to taste
2 cups uncooked rice

Serves 6 to 8

Brown the bulk pork sausage in a skillet, stirring until crumbly; drain. Combine the bulk pork sausage, smoked sausage, onions, water and duck in a saucepan. Bring to a boil and cook for 15 minutes. Season with salt and pepper. Bring to a full boil and stir in the rice. Boil for 3 to 4 minutes, stirring constantly. Reduce the heat to very low. Cook, covered, for 50 minutes or until the rice is tender and the duck is cooked through. Serve with garlic bread and coleslaw.

 Dwayne Clark

WILD GOOSE SLOW-COOKER STEW

All-purpose flour
Salt and pepper to taste
2 to 4 boneless skinless goose breasts
cut crosswise into 1- to 2-inch pieces
4 skinless goose legs
Olive oil
Butter
1 envelope onion soup mix
1 can beef broth
1 cup red wine
$1/3$ cup Worcestershire sauce
$1/3$ cup packed brown sugar
1 pound whole mushrooms
1 large onion, cut into large pieces
3 or 4 garlic cloves, chopped
1 bay leaf
1 apple, peeled and quartered
1 pound small yellow or red
potatoes, halved or quartered
1 pound carrots, cut into chunks
$1/3$ cup instant flour
$1/3$ cup milk

Serves 6 to 8

Season all-purpose flour with salt and pepper in a shallow dish. Coat the goose in the flour. Heat olive oil and butter in a skillet. Add the goose and brown on all sides. Remove the goose to a slow cooker.

Combine the soup mix, broth, wine, Worcestershire sauce and brown sugar in a bowl and mix well. Pour over the goose. Top with the mushrooms, onion, garlic, bay leaf and apple and season with salt and pepper. Cook on High for 4 to 5 hours. Add the potatoes and carrots. Cook on Low for 4 hours.

Remove the meat and vegetables with a slotted spoon to a platter and keep warm. Remove and discard the bay leaf. Whisk the instant flour and milk in a bowl. Stir into the slow cooker. Cook on High for 30 minutes or until thickened. Spoon over the meat and vegetables. Serve with a salad and hearty bread.

 Jeani Rottle

Mallards and black ducks are among the last dabbling
ducks to migrate south in the fall.

Waterfowl Winners

SIMPLE DUCK STEW

2 cans or bottles flat beer
1/4 cup Worcestershire sauce
1/3 teaspoon freshly ground
black pepper
6 garlic cloves, minced
4 cups (1 quart) duck meat, skinned,
deboned and cut into 1-inch cubes
2 tablespoons vegetable oil
1 yellow onion, coarsely chopped
2 carrots, diced
2 ribs celery, diced
2 red potatoes, diced into
1-inch cubes
1 (14-ounce) can diced tomatoes
8 cups (2 quarts) beef broth

Serves 6 to 8

Combine beer with next 3 ingredients in a glass or plastic bowl. Add duck, toss gently, cover and refrigerate for 6 to 12 hours. Remove duck from marinade; reserve marinade. Heat oil in a heavy-duty stockpot over medium-high heat. Add duck and cook until browned evenly. Add onion, carrots and celery. Cook for 3 to 5 minutes. Add unpeeled potatoes, reserved marinade, undrained tomatoes and broth. Bring to a boil, then reduce heat to low, cover and simmer until duck falls apart when poked with a spoon, about 2 to 3 hours.

SFL

Let's face it, for most of us, all of our ducks are not greenheads. This recipe works wonderfully with an assortment of ducks. The long, slow stewing process guarantees that the meat will be tender.

DUCK JAMBALAYA

1 duck, dressed and cut into quarters
2 teaspoons salt
1/2 teaspoon pepper
1/2 cup shortening
2 cups chicken broth
1/3 cup dried onion flakes
1/4 cup dried bell pepper flakes
1/4 teaspoon instant minced garlic
8 ounces bulk pork sausage
1 cup rice
1 bay leaf
1/2 teaspoon chili powder and thyme
1 teaspoon parsley flakes
1/2 cup diced cooked ham
1 cup canned whole tomatoes

Serves 4 to 6

Rub the duck with salt and pepper. Brown in hot shortening in a Dutch oven or other heavy pot over medium heat. Pour off the pan drippings. Add the broth to the pot. Cover and simmer over low heat for 1 1/2 hours or until the meat is tender. Combine the onion flakes, bell pepper flakes, garlic and 1/4 cup water in a bowl and let stand. Brown the sausage in a skillet. Drain. Add rice and rehydrated vegetables. Cook, uncovered, until rice begins to stick, stirring constantly.

Remove the duck from the pot. Add the rice mixture to broth in pot and mix well. Add the bay leaf, chili powder, thyme and parsley flakes and mix well. Cook, covered, for 10 minutes. Add the ham and tomatoes and mix gently. Place the duck on top of mixture. Cook, covered, for 10 minutes longer. Remove the bay leaf before serving.

BJC

Italian Waterfowl Sandwich

2 Canada goose breasts, skinned, deboned and fat removed
2 puddle duck breasts, skinned, deboned and fat removed
1 teaspoon chopped garlic
1 teaspoon ground cumin
1 teaspoon salt
1 teaspoon pepper
1 medium onion, sliced
2 or 3 bay leaves
5 or 6 mild or hot Italian sausage links (about 1 1/2 pounds)
1/2 to 1 cup barbecue sauce
Hot red pepper flakes (optional)
1 large onion, sliced
2 red or green bell peppers, sliced
1 to 2 teaspoons olive oil
Hoagie or Italian rolls, split

Serves 6 to 8

Cut the goose and duck breasts crosswise 1/2- to 3/4-inch thick. Rinse several times in cold water. Combine the goose, duck, garlic, cumin, salt, pepper, medium onion and bay leaves in a large saucepan and cover with water. Bring to a boil over high heat and then reduce the heat. Simmer, covered, for 2 1/2 to 3 hours, stirring occasionally; do not remove the foam.

Drain and cut the meat into bite-size pieces. Cook the sausages in a skillet for 30 to 45 minutes or until browned and cooked through; drain. Cut the sausages diagonally into bite-size pieces. Combine the goose, duck, sausage, barbecue sauce and red pepper flakes in a saucepan and cook until heated through. Sauté the large onion and bell pepper in the olive oil in a skillet until the vegetables are tender. Spoon the meat mixture into rolls and top with the bell pepper mixture.

Note: This recipe allows you to use either all duck, all goose or a combination of both with the total meat being 3 1/2 pounds. The boiling of the meat tempers and blends the flavors and the sausage adds the right amount of Italian seasoning to satisfy.

 Timothy Andrews

Duck Burgers

10 boneless duck breasts, or
4 boneless goose breasts
1 pound bulk sausage
1 green bell pepper, thinly sliced
1 red bell pepper, thinly sliced
1 bunch scallions
1 teaspoon salt
1 teaspoon pepper
1/2 teaspoon oregano
1/2 teaspoon garlic powder
1/2 teaspoon sage

Serves 16

Grind the duck with a hand or electric grinder into a large bowl. Grind the sausage into the bowl. Grind the green bell pepper, red bell pepper and scallions into the bowl. Stir in the salt, pepper, oregano, garlic powder and sage and mix well. Shape into patties. Cook the patties in a skillet over medium heat until cooked through, turning once. Add water to the skillet if needed to prevent burning. Serve on hamburger buns.

Note: This makes a great meatloaf and can also be used in tacos. These are good served between baked refrigerator biscuits instead of hamburger buns.

 Jeff Medor

CHIPOTLE DUCK BURGERS

2 boneless skinless
duck breasts, ground
1 boneless pork chop, ground
1 teaspoon chipotle Tabasco sauce
1/2 teaspoon pork and chicken
seasoning, or salt and pepper to taste
Hamburger buns or Kaiser rolls

Serves 4 to 6

Combine the duck, pork, Tabasco sauce and seasoning in a bowl and mix well. Shape into patties. Cook the patties on a hot grill until cooked through. Serve on heated buns and top with lettuce, tomato, onion and hickory barbecue sauce.

 Greg Snow

DUCK BREASTS AND BEER SANDWICH

6 to 10 duck breast half fillets,
skin removed
Salt and pepper to taste
3 tablespoons olive oil
2 yellow onions,
sliced into thick rings
2 tablespoons light brown sugar
4 garlic cloves, chopped
2 tablespoons grainy mustard
1 red bell pepper,
sliced into thin strips
Pinch of red pepper flakes
1 cup flat beer (I like to cook this
recipe with dark beer.)
4 slices provolone cheese
(or your favorite)
4 tablespoons mayonnaise
4 sandwich rolls
4 leaves lettuce
4 slices tomato

Serves 4

Season the duck breasts liberally with salt and pepper. Heat 2 tablespoons of the oil over high heat in a large skillet and sear breasts quickly on both sides, but not past rare. Remove duck and set aside.

Add remaining oil and onions to the skillet. Reduce heat to low and cook onions for 4 to 5 minutes. Add brown sugar and stir to coat. Cook until sugar has melted and coated the onions, about 3 to 4 minutes more. Add garlic and next 4 ingredients and simmer until liquid is reduced to about 1/4 cup. Return duck breasts to the pan, cover pan and heat duck breasts to medium-rare.

Remove duck and slice thinly at a diagonal. Mound with onions and pepper in pan and top with cheese; heat until melted. Spread mayonnaise on rolls and add lettuce and tomato. Mound duck, peppers, onions and cheese onto tomato.

SFL

How's that for an attention grabber? Well-seasoned duck breasts simmered in beer with sweet onions and garlic—oh my! I recommend enjoying this recipe with a full chilled tankard of your favorite foaming ambrosia.

Goose Quesadillas

1 envelope fajita seasoning
4 boneless skinless goose breasts, cut
lengthwise into thin strips
2 tablespoons olive oil
1 large onion, sliced
1 bell pepper, sliced
12 flour tortillas
1 package shredded Mexican
blend cheese
1 package shredded Pepper
Jack cheese

Serves 6

Sprinkle one-half of the fajita seasoning over the goose in a bowl and toss to coat. Heat 1 tablespoon of the olive oil in a skillet. Add the goose and sauté to medium-rare. Remove to a bowl. Heat the remaining 1 tablespoon olive oil in the skillet. Add the onion, bell pepper and remaining fajita seasoning and sauté for 4 minutes.

Arrange 6 of the tortillas in a shallow baking pan coated with nonstick cooking spray. Top each with equal portions of the goose, onion mixture, Mexican cheese and Pepper Jack cheese. Cover with the remaining tortillas and press firmly. Bake at 350 degrees for 10 minutes.

Cut each quesadilla into quarters. Serve with guacamole, sour cream, sliced jalapeño chiles and shredded lettuce.

 Jason Thornton

Teal Quesadillas

6 teal breast fillets
Salt to taste
Black pepper to taste
Cayenne pepper to taste
Garlic powder to taste
Onion powder to taste
2 tablespoons butter or margarine
1 1/4 cups pico de gallo
1/2 bag baby spinach, stems removed
8 flour tortillas
2 cups (8 ounces) shredded
Monterey Jack cheese
2 cups (8 ounces) shredded Cheddar
cheese or American cheese

Serves 4

Cut the duck into 1/4- to 1/2-inch strips and season lightly with salt, black pepper, cayenne pepper, garlic powder and onion powder. Melt the butter in a skillet. Add the duck and sauté to medium-rare. Add the pico de gallo and sauté until the duck is medium. Add the spinach and sauté just until the spinach begins to wilt. Remove from the heat.

Arrange 4 tortillas in a shallow baking pan. Top each with equal portions of the Monterey Jack cheese. Drain the goose mixture and spoon equal portions over the Monterey Jack cheese. Top with equal portions of the Cheddar cheese and cover with the remaining tortillas. Bake at 300 degrees for 20 minutes, pressing down on the quesadillas with a spaula occasionally.

Cut each quesadilla into 4 to 6 triangles and serve with salsa, guacamole and sour cream.

Note: These are fabulous and a hit with everyone who has tried them.

 Richard Walton

SNOW GOOSE TOSTADAS

3 or 4 snow goose breasts, or
equivalent amount of duck breasts,
skin removed
3 ounces tequila (optional)
$1/4$ cup sweet-and-sour mix
2 tablespoons lime juice
1 tablespoon granulated sugar
1 teaspoon lemon pepper
$1/3$ cup vegetable oil
4 flat corn tortillas, fried
$1^1/2$ cups cooked black beans, warm
2 cups lettuce, shredded
$1/2$ cup red onion, finely diced
1 red bell pepper, cut into thin rings
1 cup shredded Pepper Jack cheese
2 firm, ripe avocados, sliced
2 cups tomato salsa
2 fresh limes, quartered
2 large tomatoes,
each cut into 4 wedges
4 sprigs of cilantro

Serves 4

In a nonreactive container, combine goose breasts with next 5 ingredients and half the oil. Refrigerate for 1 to 2 hours. Pat dry and discard marinade.

Heat remaining oil in a large skillet over medium-high heat. Add goose breasts and cook until medium-brown on one side. Flip over and cook other side until medium-rare. Remove from pan and keep warm.

Assemble tostada. Place tortilla on plate. Top with beans, lettuce and onion. Thinly slice goose and fan over top of lettuce. Add red bell pepper, cheese, avocado and salsa. Garnish with lime and tomato wedges and top with sprig of cilantro.

SFL

peckled geese make for some great table fare. They're tender, just the right size, and in my opinion, the best tasting goose. On the other hand, snow geese can be a bit more pronounced in flavor. I'm told that this is because they dig deep into the decomposed matter to get at the roots of tuberous plants. I'm not sure that that's the real deal, but I do know that when I shoot snow geese early in the season in Manitoba, they taste great, about like mallard. Apparently, their diet changes once they cross the border. Have no fear, snow geese are still fit for the table. Here's how I make them taste their best.

Up the Creek *(2001)*
Richard (Dick) Plasschaert

International Artist of the Year —2001

Accuracy and attention to detail are Plasschaert trademarks. His original work and limited-edition prints are highly sought after by collectors. His signature on a state of conservation stamp ensures strong sales.

Dick Plasschaert's wildlife art career took off after his entry of *Two Mallards in Flight* was selected for the 1980–81 Federal Duck Stamp. Overnight, he joined the ranks of America's top wildlife artists. Plasschaert likes to say that it took him twenty years to become an overnight success.

In addition to the 1980–81 Federal Stamp, he was chosen as the artist for the "first" North Dakota Duck Stamp, the "first" North Carolina Duck Stamp, the "first" New Hampshire Duck Stamp, the "first" Minnesota Conservation Federal Stamp and print, the Louisiana Turkey Stamp, and the 1988 New York Duck Stamp.

BAKED CHERRY DUCK

1 (4-pound) duck, cut into quarters
Salt and pepper to taste
2 tablespoons butter
2 tablespoons dry sherry
1/4 teaspoon crushed garlic
1 can pitted Bing cherries, drained
and juice reserved
2 teaspoons cornstarch
1 teaspoon tomato paste
1 bay leaf
Hot cooked white or brown rice

Serves 4

Season the duck with salt and pepper. Melt the butter in a skillet over medium heat. Add the duck and brown on all sides; drain. Pour the sherry over the duck and remove the duck to a baking dish.

Add the garlic and cherries to the skillet and cook for 2 to 3 minutes, stirring frequently. Mix the reserved cherry juice, cornstarch and tomato paste in a small bowl and add to the skillet. Add the bay leaf. Cook until thickened, stirring constantly. Pour over the duck in the baking dish. Bake, covered, at 350 degrees for 45 minutes or until the duck is cooked through. Remove and discard the bay leaf. Serve over white or brown rice.

 Don Ball

CANDY CHESAPEAKE BAY CANVASBACKS

8 slices bacon
1/2 cup (1 stick) butter or margarine
1 large sweet onion, sliced
2 cups mushrooms, sliced
1/2 cup canola oil
2 cups self-rising flour
1/4 teaspoon pepper
2 tablespoons Mrs. Dash seasoning
2 canvasbacks, split,
deboned and skinned
4 sweet potatoes, cooked, peeled
and sliced
3/4 cup packed brown sugar
1 1/2 tablespoons lemon juice
1/4 teaspoon salt
2 tablespoons butter or margarine

Serves 4

Cook the bacon a large skillet until crisp. Remove the bacon with tongs to paper towels to drain; crumble. Add 1/2 cup butter to the drippings in the skillet. Add the onion and mushrooms and sauté until the vegetables are tender. Remove with a slotted spoon to a bowl.

Add the canola oil to the skillet. Mix the flour, pepper and seasoning together. Dredge the duck in the flour mixture to coat. Cook the duck in the skillet over medium heat for 7 to 10 minutes per side or until golden brown.

Arrange the sweet potatoes in a 9×13-inch baking dish. Sprinkle with the brown sugar, lemon juice and salt and dot with 2 tablespoons butter. Bake, uncovered, at 375 degrees for 20 minutes.

Arrange the ducks over the sweet potatoes and top with the onion mixture and bacon. Bake, covered, at 375 degrees for 10 to 15 minutes.

 Talbert Dunn

PLUM BRANDY SPECIAL

3 tablespoons plum preserves
3 tablespoons apricot preserves
1/2 teaspoon anise seeds
Pinch of garlic powder
3 pinches each of salt and pepper
2 tablespoons barbecue sauce
2 tablespoons ketchup
1 tablespoon whole grain mustard
1/2 cup brandy
1 whole duck
1 cup water or apple juice

Serves 4

Mix the plum preserves, apricot preserves, anise seeds, garlic powder, salt, pepper, barbecue sauce, ketchup, mustard and brandy in a small saucepan. Simmer over low heat, stirring occasionally.

Place the duck in a shallow roasting pan and pour the water around the duck. Roast at 350 degrees for 15 minutes. Brush the brandy mixture over the entire duck. Roast at 350 degrees until cooked through.

Note: This recipe is best enjoyed when using a clay cooking dish with a lid. The dish must be soaked in water for at least 30 minutes before adding the duck.

 Brian Tunge

DUCK WITH CRANBERRY-HONEY SAUCE AND PINEAPPLE-WILD RICE STUFFING

Pineapple-Wild Rice Stuffing
Neck and giblets of 1 duck
Salt to taste
1 small onion, chopped
1 small green bell pepper, chopped
2 cups chopped fresh mushrooms
1/4 cup (1/2 stick) butter
1 (8-ounce) can crushed pineapple
1 box long grain and wild rice mix, prepared

Duck
1 large wild duck
Vinegar and salt for marinating
1/2 cup cranberry juice
3 tablespoons honey
1 envelope brown gravy mix

Serves 4

The Stuffing: Simmer the duck neck and giblets in a saucepan of lightly salted water for 1 hour or until tender. Drain, reserving 1/2 cup of the cooking liquid. Chop the neck meat and giblets. Sauté the onion, bell pepper and mushrooms in the butter in a saucepan until tender. Stir in the pineapple. Add the cooked rice and neck and giblet meat and mix well.

The Duck: Marinate the whole duck in a mixture of water, vinegar and salt in a bowl for several hours. Drain the duck and pat dry. Stuff the duck cavity with the rice stuffing. Truss to seal the opening. Place the duck on a rack in a shallow roasting pan. Roast at 325 degrees for 1 1/2 hours.

Combine the cranberry juice, honey, gravy mix and 1/2 cup reserved cooking liquid and mix well. Brush over the duck. Roast for 30 minutes longer or until a rich brown color and cooked through. Brush with the remaining cranberry mixture. Serve with any remaining rice stuffing.

 Hal Griffin

ITALIAN WILD MALLARD OPEN FACE

4 boneless skinless
mallard breasts
1 cup balsamic vinaigrette
1 teaspoon garlic salt
1 teaspoon pepper
1 cup all-purpose flour
1 tablespoon olive oil
2 large red onions, cut into
1/2-inch slices
8 ounces large mushrooms, cut into
1/4-inch slices
1 (14-ounce) can quartered
artichoke hearts, drained
1 tablespoon olive oil
3/4 cup (about) spaghetti sauce
2 tomatoes, cut into 1/4-inch slices
1 teaspoon dried oregano
2 teaspoons basil
1 1/2 cups (6 ounces) shredded
mozzarella cheese

Serves 4

Pound the duck breasts between sheets of waxed paper with a meat mallet to 1/4-inch thick. Pour the vinaigrette over the duck in a shallow dish. Marinate in the refrigerator for 1 hour. Drain and discard the marinade. Sprinkle the duck with the garlic salt and pepper and coat in the flour.

Heat 1 tablespoon olive oil in a large skillet. Add the onions and sauté until tender. Remove the onions with a slotted spoon to a bowl. Add the mushrooms and artichokes to the skillet and sauté until tender. Remove to a bowl. Add 1 tablespoon olive oil to the skillet. Add the duck and sauté until golden brown on both sides.

Arrange the duck in a shallow nonstick baking pan. Spread 1 tablespoon spaghetti sauce over each duck breast. Top each duck breast with equal portions of the onions, tomatoes, mushrooms and artichokes. Spread 2 tablespoons spaghetti sauce over the top of each and sprinkle with the oregano, basil and cheese. Bake at 375 degrees for 20 minutes.

Note: You may substitute goose breast for the duck breast and it will be equally good.

 Fred Muetze

Ducks Unlimited® was founded by a group of waterfowl hunters more than seventy years ago. Today 90 percent of DU™ members are hunters.

Apples 'n' Teal

3 tablespoons margarine
4 to 6 teal, deboned and
cut into pieces
2 Granny Smith apples, cut into
1/2-inch slices
1 cup sliced celery (1/2-inch thick)
1 onion, finely chopped
1/2 cup dry white wine
1/2 cup chicken broth
2 tablespoons cornstarch
2 tablespoons cold water
1/2 cup heavy cream
1/2 teaspoon salt
1/2 teaspoon pepper
Sugar
2 red apples, cut into 1/2-inch slices
3 tablespoons margarine

Serves 4 to 6

Melt 3 tablespoons margarine in a Dutch oven. Add the teal and brown on all sides. Remove the teal with a slotted spoon to a bowl. Add the Granny Smith apples, celery and onion to the Dutch oven and sauté over medium-low heat until tender. Stir in the wine and broth. Cook over medium heat for 5 minutes, stirring occasionally. Stir in the teal. Bake, covered, at 350 degrees for 40 minutes or until the teal is cooked through.

Remove the teal with a slotted spoon to a platter and keep warm. Strain the cooking liquid through a wire mesh strainer into a bowl and return the liquid to the Dutch oven. Discard the solids. Dissolve the cornstarch in the cold water in a small bowl. Stir into the cooking liquid. Cook over medium heat until thick and bubbly, stirring constantly. Reduce the heat to low and stir in the cream, salt and pepper. Cook until heated through. Remove from the heat and keep warm.

Sprinkle sugar over the red apple slices on waxed paper. Melt 3 tablespoons margarine in a skillet over medium-low heat. Add the apples and cook until golden brown on both sides. Remove the apples to a serving platter and top with the teal. Pour the sauce over the teal and serve.

 David Reinhardt

CANVASBACK WITH BLUE CHEESE, MUSHROOMS AND ASPARAGUS

4 canvasback breasts, skin on or off
Olive oil
1 tablespoon Italian seasoning
Salt and pepper to taste
1/3 cup crumbled blue cheese
2 tablespoons breadcrumbs
12 asparagus spears, blanched in
salted water and cooled
4 fresh sprigs of rosemary
3 tablespoons butter
2 cups fresh mushrooms, quartered
2 garlic cloves, minced
2 teaspoons Worcestershire sauce
1 cup tomato, seeded and diced

Serves 4

On a flat surface, butterfly each duck breast, leaving a "hinge" connecting the two halves. Rub duck liberally on both sides with olive oil. Season with Italian seasoning, salt and pepper. Place duck breasts outside down on a flat surface. Combine blue cheese with breadcrumbs and spread on middle of duck. Top with asparagus and rosemary sprig and roll breasts up snugly around asparagus. Arrange rolled duck breasts seam side down in a lightly greased baking dish. Place dish in a preheated 450-degree oven and cook for 10 to 12 minutes or until cheese is melted.

While duck is cooking, heat butter in a medium skillet over medium-high heat. Add mushrooms and garlic and sauté for 5 minutes. Add Worcestershire sauce and sauté until mushrooms are tender.

Remove duck from oven. Arrange on plates. Top with mushrooms and tomato.

SFL

Canvasbacks are large, strong ducks that can be a bit dark and lean, depending on where they feed. Here's a canvasback recipe you're gonna love. Invite the boss over for dinner.

Apple Pie Duck with Apple and Hot Sausage Stuffing

1 tablespoon cider vinegar
1 teaspoon salt
1 teaspoon pepper
1 teaspoon nutmeg
1 tablespoon cinnamon
1 tablespoon sugar
4 duck breasts
1 tablespoon butter
1 cup chopped green bell pepper
1 cup chopped yellow onion
2 tablespoons chopped garlic
2 McIntosh apples, chopped
8 ounces hot Italian sausage,
casings removed
1 package stuffing mix

Serves 4

Sprinkle the vinegar, salt, pepper, nutmeg, cinnamon and sugar evenly over the duck in a bowl. Melt the butter in a skillet over medium heat. Add the bell pepper, onion and garlic and sauté until the vegetables are tender. Add the apples and sauté until tender. Add the duck and sausage and cook until the sausage and duck are cooked through. Remove the duck with tongs to a platter and keep warm. Prepare the stuffing mix using the package directions. Add the stuffing to the skillet and mix well. Serve the stuffing with the duck.

 Chad Pomeroy

Duck Breast with Asparagus and Artichoke Pasta

4 duck breasts
1/4 cup olive oil
4 garlic cloves, chopped
1 pound asparagus, chopped
1 (16-ounce) can marinated
artichoke hearts, drained
2 cups cherry tomatoes
1/4 cup chopped fresh basil
1 jar Greek olives, drained
16 ounces bow-tie pasta, cooked
and drained

Serves 4

Arrange the duck breasts in a baking dish. Bake at 325 degrees for 40 minutes or until cooked through. Remove the skin and bones when cool and chop the meat.

Heat the olive oil in a skillet. Add the garlic and sauté until tender. Stir in the asparagus, artichokes, tomatoes and basil. Simmer over low heat for 30 minutes. Stir in the olives and duck. Add the pasta and toss to mix. Cook just until heated through.

 Greg Konle

ALMOND DUCK

1 egg
2 tablespoons milk
1/2 cup ground almonds
1/4 teaspoon sage
Salt and pepper to taste
2 boneless skinless duck breasts
Olive oil

Serves 2

Beat the egg in a bowl and stir in the milk. Combine the almonds, sage, salt and pepper in a shallow dish and mix well. Dip the duck in the egg mixture and coat in the almonds. Heat a skillet and coat with a small amount of olive oil. Add the duck and fry for 5 minutes per side or until golden brown and cooked through.

 Dave Engstrom

BULL'S DUCK-BERRY BAKE

4 duck breasts
1 can whole cranberry sauce
1 small bottle French salad dressing
1 envelope onion soup mix
1/4 cup white wine

Serves 4

Arrange the duck in a lightly greased 9×13-inch baking dish. Combine the cranberry sauce, salad dressing, soup mix and wine in a bowl and mix well. Pour over the duck. Bake at 350 degrees for 1 hour or until the duck is cooked through.

 Bob Bullinger

CANDIED DUCK

2 cups all-purpose flour
1 tablespoon seasoned salt
1 tablespoon pepper
1 tablespoon garlic
1 to 2 pounds duck breasts
1/4 cup vegetable oil
1 bell pepper, coarsely chopped
1 large onion, coarsely chopped
2 cups packed brown sugar
Favorite steak sauce

Serves 4

Mix the flour, seasoned salt, pepper and garlic powder in a shallow dish. Coat the duck in the flour mixture. Heat the oil in a skillet. Add the duck and brown quickly on all sides. Layer the bell pepper and onion in a 9×13-inch baking pan and top with the duck. Spread the brown sugar over the duck. Drizzle with steak sauce. Cover tightly with foil. Bake at 300 degrees for 2 to 2 1/2 hours or until the duck is cooked through.

Note: It is extremely important that you seal the foil tightly so that the steam produced by the vegetables does not escape since it helps tenderize the duck.

 Rhonda White

BUTT'S UP DUCK

2 cups water
1 teaspoon thyme
1 teaspoon garlic powder
1 wild duck, dressed
8 ounces bulk pork sausage

Serves 4

Mix the water, thyme and garlic powder in a bowl. Pour into a shallow roasting pan. Poke three holes into each breast of the duck with a small sharp knife, being certain to penetrate the cavity. Stuff the cavity with the sausage.

Place the duck breast side down in the roasting pan. Insert four wooden picks into the sides of the duck to prevent it from rolling in the pan.

Bake, covered, at 350 degrees for 1 hour or until a meat thermometer inserted in the breast registers 180 degrees.

Make gravy with the pan drippings, if desired.

 Ryan Ostrander

One of the main problems with roasting wild duck is keeping the meat from drying out. Common poultry recipes roast birds breast up. However, roasting ducks breast up causes what little juice is present to evaporate, leaving the meat dry. The solution? Butt's Up Duck.

CHIPOTLE DUCK PASTA

1/4 cup olive oil
1 pound boneless duck meat, cut into small pieces
1 (7-ounce) can chipotle chiles in adobo sauce
Sliced portobello mushrooms or favorite mushrooms
1 cup dry white wine
2 cups heavy cream or half-and-half
1/2 cup (2 ounces) grated Parmesan cheese
Angel hair pasta, cooked and drained
Salt and pepper to taste

Serves 4

Heat the olive oil in a skillet. Add the duck and sauté until browned on all sides. Stir in the chiles, mushrooms and wine. Simmer until the mushrooms are tender. Stir in the cream and bring to a boil. Reduce the heat to low and stir in the cheese. Cook until the cheese is melted.

Serve over pasta and season with salt and pepper.

 Patrick Gibson

DUCK BREAST WITH CRAN-RAISIN CHUTNEY

1/4 cup dried cranberries
1/4 cup raisins
1/4 cup dried cherries
1/4 cup orange juice
1/2 cup port
1/4 cup white wine
4 boneless duck breasts (about 1 1/2 pounds)
1 teaspoon olive oil

Serves 8

Combine the first 6 ingredients in a bowl and mix well. Let stand for 2 hours. Drain, reserving the liquid. Chop the fruit. Cut a deep slit in each duck breast to form a pocket. Stuff the pockets with the fruit chutney and secure each opening with 2 wooden picks.

Heat the olive oil in a skillet. Add the duck, skin side down, and cook for 10 minutes. Turn and cook until the duck is cooked through. Pour the reserved liquid over the duck and simmer for 3 minutes. Remove the duck to a cutting board and let stand for 2 minutes. Remove the wooden picks and slice the duck on the diagonal. Arrange duck breasts in a fan shape on serving plates and spoon the pan sauce over the top. Serve with any remaining chutney.

Note: This is a nice recipe for serving duck breasts with a dinner for friends or a romantic evening for two. I like to serve this dish with wild rice; the nutty flavor compliments the duck well.

 Nicholas Walker

DUCK DIJONNAISE

1 boneless skinless duck breast
Freshly ground sea salt to taste
Freshly ground pepper to taste
All-purpose flour for dredging
1 cup dry white wine
2 tablespoons minced garlic
2 tablespoons minced shallot
1/2 cup chicken stock
1/2 cup cream
1/2 cup Dijon mustard
1 teaspoon salt
1 teaspoon cracked pepper

Serves 2

Season the duck with sea salt and ground pepper and dredge lightly in flour. Fry in a nonstick skillet until golden brown on both sides. Stir in the wine, garlic and shallot. Simmer over medium-high heat until the liquid is almost evaporated. Stir in the stock and cream and bring to a boil. Reduce the heat and simmer for 8 minutes.

Stir in the Dijon mustard, 1 teaspoon salt and 1 teaspoon pepper. Simmer for 2 minutes.

Note: This is a good recipe for using "scrap" ducks like blackjack, spoonies, or widgeon.

 Christopher Stonesifer

HOTSHOT DUCKS

Injector Cajun duck marinade
1 capful liquid crab boil
4 boneless duck breasts, cut in
half horizontally
Coarsely ground black pepper
1 onion, sliced
1 jalapeño chile or bell pepper, sliced
Olive oil
8 ounces (50- to 60-count)
peeled shrimp
Salt to taste

Serves 8

Mix the duck marinade and crab boil in a bowl and pour into a meat injector. Inject the marinade evenly into the duck. Coat the duck in pepper.

Sauté the onion and jalapeño chile in a nonstick skillet until golden brown and tender. Heat olive oil in a skillet. Add the duck and sear for 2 to 4 minutes per side. Arrange half the duck in a baking pan and top with the shrimp. Spoon half the onion mixture over the shrimp. Season lightly with salt. Top with the remaining duck and spoon the remaining onion mixture over the duck.

Bake, covered with foil, at 350 degrees for 10 to 15 minutes. Uncover and bake for 10 to 15 minutes longer or until the shrimp turn pink and the duck is cooked through.

Serve with hot buttered pistolettes or other rolls.

 Michael Galliano

CURRY CAJUN DUCK WITH WINE

2 tablespoons butter, melted
1/3 cup honey
3 tablespoons mustard
2 tablespoons lemon juice
2 garlic gloves, minced
3 tablespoons water
2 to 3 teaspoons curry powder
2 to 3 teaspoons Cajun seasoning
1/3 cup crushed pineapple
6 duck breasts
Hot cooked brown rice

Serves 6

Combine the butter, honey, mustard, lemon juice, garlic, water, curry powder, Cajun seasoning and pineapple in a bowl and mix well. Pour into a 9×13-inch baking pan. Add the duck breasts and turn once to coat.

Bake at 350 degrees for 30 minutes or until the duck is cooked through. Serve over brown rice and garnish with butter lettuce leaves and candied apple slices.

 Ben Gallup

DUCKS GONE DIXIE

3 green tomatoes, cut into
1/4-inch slices
1 cup cider vinegar
1/4 cup water
1/4 cup chopped fresh basil
1 tablespoon sugar
1 cup sour cream
1 cup buttermilk
1 tablespoon minced garlic
2 tablespoons cider vinegar
1 teaspoon Worcestershire sauce
2 tablespoons finely chopped
fresh basil
1/2 cup crumbled blue cheese
Salt and pepper to taste
4 boneless mallard breasts
1 package hardwood-smoked bacon

Serves 4 to 8

Place the tomatoes in a bowl. Mix 1 cup vinegar, the water, 1/4 cup basil and the sugar in a bowl and pour over the tomatoes. Marinate for 30 minutes. Pour into a colander and let drain for 5 minutes.

Whisk the sour cream, buttermilk, garlic, 2 tablespoons vinegar, the Worcestershire sauce and 2 tablespoons basil in a bowl. Stir in the blue cheese and season with salt and pepper.

Season the duck with salt and pepper. Wrap the bacon slices around the duck breasts, completely covering each. Secure the bacon with a wooden pick on each side.

Heat a skillet over medium-high heat. Add the duck and cook until the bacon is crisp one side. Turn and cook until the bacon is crisp and the duck is medium-rare. Remove the duck to paper towels to drain.

Slice the duck thinly and serve over the tomatoes. Drizzle the blue cheese dressing over the top.

 Walter Bundy

DUCK BLIND COOKING WITH BALSAMIC BERRY SAUCE

4 large duck breast fillets,
skin on or off
Salt and pepper
1 tablespoon olive oil
1/4 cup balsamic vinegar
1/2 cup cheap red wine
2 garlic cloves, minced
1 tablespoon plum preserves
(or brown sugar)
1 tablespoon fresh rosemary leaves,
minced (optional)
3 tablespoons cold butter,
cut into 3 pieces
1 1/2 cups fresh berries
(frozen will do also)

Serves 4

Season duck breasts with salt and pepper. Heat oil in a large skillet over medium-high heat. Add duck breasts and brown on one side. Flip over and cook for 1 minute. Add balsamic vinegar, wine, garlic and preserves. Remove duck breasts when just medium-rare and keep warm. Add rosemary to skillet and reduce liquid to about 1/4 cup. Taste liquid and add more vinegar or plum preserves to suit your taste. Too sour? Add more preserves. Too sweet? Add more vinegar.

Whisk in butter until melted. Stir in berries. Slice duck and arrange on plates. Spoon sauce over.

SFL

You can watch a video clip of this recipe at www.MyOutdoorTV.com! It's fast, hot, easy, and delicious!

DUCK ITALIANO WITH POLENTA

8 ounces sliced mushrooms
1/4 cup (1/2 stick) butter
1/4 cup marsala
4 duck breasts
3 cans crushed tomatoes
6 garlic cloves, chopped
1/2 cup chopped fresh basil
1 tablespoon anise seeds
6 cups water
1 teaspoon salt
1 1/2 cups cornmeal
1 cup (4 ounces) grated
Parmesan cheese
6 thin slices mozzarella cheese

Serves 6

Sauté the mushrooms in the butter in a skillet until golden brown and tender. Stir in the wine. Cook until reduced. Remove to a slow cooker. Stir in the duck, tomatoes, garlic, basil and anise seeds. Cook on High for 3 hours. Remove the duck to a cutting board. Remove the meat from the bones and cut the meat into small pieces. Return the meat to the slow cooker and cook on Low for 1 hour.

Bring the water to a boil in a saucepan and add the salt. Reduce the heat and stir in the cornmeal gradually. Cook over low heat for 25 minutes or until thickened, stirring frequently. Stir in the Parmesan cheese gradually. Cook until the cheese is melted, stirring constantly. Spread several tablespoons of polenta over each of six serving plates and top each with one slice of mozzarella cheese. Top with equal portions of the duck mixture.

 Roger Eade

ANATRA AL RAGÙ (DUCK WITH MEAT SAUCE)

8 small skinless duck breasts
1 cup seasoned flour
Olive oil
8 ounces ground beef
1/2 cup dry red wine
8 russet potatoes, peeled and
cut in half
8 cups tomato sauce
Salt and pepper to taste
16 ounces pasta, cooked and drained

Serves 8

Coat the duck in the flour. Cover the bottom of a large skillet with olive oil and heat. Add the duck and sear on both sides. Remove the duck to paper towels.

Add the ground beef to the skillet and cook, stirring until crumbly; drain. Remove the ground beef to a bowl.

Add the wine to the skillet and cook, stirring constantly and scraping up any browned bits from the bottom of the pan.

Return the ground beef and duck to the skillet. Add the potatoes and tomato sauce. Cook over medium-low heat for 1 hour or until the duck is cooked through. Season with salt and pepper. Serve over the pasta.

 Sebastiano Conigliaro

DUCK BREASTS WITH WILD MUSHROOMS AND FIGS

14 fresh or dried black figs, cut in
half lengthwise
2 cups dry red wine
1³/4 cups chicken broth
1¹/2 cinnamon sticks
¹/4 cup (¹/2 stick) butter
¹/3 cup finely chopped shallots
1¹/4 pounds fresh mushrooms
(portobello, chanterelle, oyster and
shiitake), thinly sliced
1 teaspoon finely chopped
fresh ginger
¹/4 cup chicken broth
3 tablespoons chopped fresh chives
16 fresh or dried black figs
¹/4 cup honey
4 boneless duck breasts
Salt and pepper to taste
1 tablespoon butter
1 tablespoon olive oil

Serves 4

Combine 14 figs, the wine, 1³/4 cups broth and the cinnamon sticks in a saucepan. Simmer over medium heat for 30 minutes or to a sauce consistency, stirring occasionally. Strain the sauce through a wire mesh strainer into a bowl, pressing to remove all of the liquid. Discard the solids.

Melt ¹/4 cup butter in a large skillet over medium heat. Add the shallots and sauté for 3 to 4 minutes or until tender. Add the mushrooms and ginger and sauté for 3 to 4 minutes or until the mushrooms are tender. Add ¹/4 cup broth and simmer until most of the liquid has evaporated. Stir in the chives. Remove from the heat and keep warm.

Arrange 16 figs in a small baking dish and drizzle with the honey. Bake at 450 degrees for 10 to 12 minutes or until the figs are tender and the honey is slightly caramelized.

Season the duck with salt and pepper. Heat 1 tablespoon butter and the olive oil in a heavy skillet over medium heat. Add the duck, skin side down. Cook for 5 minutes. Turn and cook for 3 minutes for medium-rare. Remove the duck to a cutting board and slice thinly.

Divide the mushroom mixture among 4 serving plates and top with the duck. Reheat the fig sauce and spoon over the duck. Arrange 4 caramelized figs on each plate and serve.

 John Ferrario

PAN-FRIED MALLARD BREAST

3 tablespoons olive oil
8 boneless skinless
mallard breasts
2 onions, chopped
2 tablespoons brown sugar
2 tablespoons mustard
3 tablespoons honey
Dash of pepper

Serves 4 to 6

Heat the olive oil in a skillet. Add the duck and brown on both sides. Remove the duck to a plate. Add the onions to the skillet and sauté until golden brown. Stir in the brown sugar, mustard, honey and pepper. Cook over medium heat until thickened, stirring constantly. Return the duck to the skillet and cook for 5 minutes or until the duck is cooked through.

 Kevin Kolenski

DELICIOUS MINT ORANGE DUCK

1 1/2 tablespoons butter
1/2 red onion, chopped
1/2 cup fresh orange juice
2/3 cup chicken broth
1 1/2 tablespoons orange liqueur
1 1/2 teaspoons cornstarch
1 1/2 teaspoons cold water
3 to 5 duck breast fillets
Salt and pepper to taste
1 1/2 teaspoons olive oil
2 cups hot cooked rice
1 orange, peeled and sliced crosswise
1 tablespoon (or more) finely
chopped fresh mint

Serves 2

Melt half the butter in a saucepan over medium-high heat. Add the onion and sauté until tender. Stir in the orange juice, broth and orange liqueur. Simmer until reduced to 1/2 cup. Dissolve the cornstarch in the cold water in a small bowl. Stir into the orange mixture gradually and cook until thickened, stirring constantly. Remove from the heat and keep warm.

Season the duck with salt and pepper. Heat the remaining butter and the olive oil in a skillet over medium-high heat. Brown the duck on both sides and cook to medium-rare. Remove to a cutting board and slice.

Divide the rice between two serving plates and top with equal portions of the duck. Stir the orange slices and mint into the orange sauce and season with salt and pepper. Spoon over the duck and serve.

 Criss Rush

DUCK PARMESAN

4 to 6 boneless skinless duck breasts
1 egg
2 cups Italian-style bread crumbs
Olive oil
2 garlic cloves, minced
1 onion, chopped
1 green bell pepper, chopped
8 ounces mushrooms, sliced
1 teaspoon salt
1 teaspoon pepper
1 (16-ounce) jar spaghetti sauce
2 cups (8 ounces) grated
Parmesan cheese

Serves 4 to 6

Cut the duck into 1/4-inch strips on a cutting board and then pound with a meat mallet to 1/4 inch thick. Beat the egg in a bowl. Dip the duck strips in the egg and coat in the bread crumbs.

Heat a small amount of olive oil in a skillet. Add the garlic, onion and bell pepper and sauté until the vegetables are tender. Add the duck and sauté until golden brown. Add the mushrooms and sauté until tender. Stir in the salt and pepper.

Layer the duck mixture, spaghetti sauce and cheese one-third at a time in a rectangular baking dish. Bake at 375 degrees for 30 to 45 minutes or until heated through and the cheese is melted.

 Margaret Rathje

PAN-SEARED DUCK BREAST WITH RASPBERRIES

4 boneless duck breasts
Kosher salt and freshly ground
pepper to taste
1 tablespoon olive oil
1/2 teaspoon butter
2 fresh sage leaves, or 2 pinches
dried rubbed sage
1/4 cup merlot or other dry red wine
1/4 cup chicken broth
1/3 cup seedless raspberry jam
5 1/2 teaspoons butter
Hot cooked wild rice

Serves 4

Score the duck skin only with a sharp knife. Season lightly with salt and pepper. Heat the olive oil in a skillet over high heat. Add the duck skin side down and cook for 3 minutes. Turn the duck and reduce the heat to medium-low. Cook for 3 minutes. Remove the duck to a plate and drain the skillet.

Add 1/2 teaspoon butter, the sage and wine to the skillet. Cook, stirring constantly and scraping up any browned bits from the bottom of the pan. Stir in the broth and jam gradually. Add the duck and any drippings to the skillet. Cook over low heat to medium-rare. Remove the duck to a cutting board and let stand for a few minutes. Cook the sauce in the skillet until reduced by one-half. Stir in 5 1/2 teaspoons butter gradually. Cook until the butter is melted, stirring constantly.

Slice the duck and serve over wild rice. Top with the sauce and garnish with fresh raspberries and chopped parsley.

 Doehne Duckworth

DUCK BREAST WITH RED WINE AND MUSHROOM SAUCE

4 boneless skinless duck breasts
Salt and pepper to taste
1/4 cup (1/2 stick) butter
2 tablespoons olive oil
2 cups sliced mushrooms
2 garlic cloves, minced
1/2 cup red wine

Serves 2

Season the duck lightly with salt and pepper. Heat 2 tablespoons of the butter and 1 tablespoon of the olive oil in a skillet over medium-high heat. Add the duck and cook for 3 minutes per side or until cooked through. Remove the duck to an ovenproof plate and keep warm in a low oven.

Heat the remaining butter and olive oil in the skillet over medium heat. Add the mushrooms and sauté for 2 minutes. Add the garlic and sauté for 2 minutes or until the vegetables are tender. Add the wine and cook until reduced by one-quarter and slightly thickened. Season with salt and pepper.

Slice the duck diagonally. Arrange in a fan shape on 2 serving plates and spoon the sauce over the top. Serve with mashed potatoes or white rice.

 Todd George

Quick Corn Relish
2 tablespoons olive oil
2 cups fresh or frozen uncooked
corn kernels
1/4 cup onion, finely diced
1/3 cup bell pepper (any color),
finely diced
1 jalapeño chile, seeded
and minced
2 garlic cloves, minced
2 tablespoons sugar
1/4 cup cider vinegar
1/4 teaspoon kosher salt
Pinch of black pepper

Duck Breasts
4 large duck breasts
Olive oil
Salt and pepper to taste
1/2 cup chicken broth

Serves 4

The Relish: Heat oil in a medium skillet over medium-high heat. Add corn and next 4 ingredients. Cook for 4 to 5 minutes, then sprinkle sugar over and stir. Cook for 2 minutes more. Add vinegar, salt and pepper and cook for 2 to 3 minutes.

The Duck: Rub duck breasts with olive oil, salt and pepper. Heat 2 tablespoons olive oil in a large skillet over medium-high heat. Brown breasts on one side, flip over and cook for 2 minutes more. Add chicken broth to pan and cook until breasts are medium-rare, about 130 degrees at the center. Allow to rest for a few minutes, slice diagonally and top with warm corn relish.

SFL

In many parts of the country, like my own backyard in Northern California, some duck hunters have a problem with shooting gadwall. "Oh, man . . . all we saw were gaddies today. Hopefully, we'll get some good ducks next time." One of the guys I hunt with maintained for years that our Northern California gadwalls head over to Nevada and pig out on snails, giving their meat a distinctive snail-like flavor. Hey, who hasn't heard about what a Nevada snail will do to a perfectly good duck? I believe what he said was, "I wouldn't feed a gadwall to my dog." So, I finally told him to put up or shut up. I brought along a portable burner, a pan, some oil, salt, pepper, and a little sauce. I cooked a gadwall breast and a mallard breast—seasoned, rubbed, seared, and sauced. Guess what? John picked out the gadwall as the mallard. Now, it could have gone either way because the finished product is really close. I just got lucky. It did take him a few tastes to choose the winner. The point is—finally—that those gadwalls you've been less than thrilled with might just surprise you. Give 'em another try.

2 to 4 cups chopped pecans
1/2 cup finely chopped white onion
1 green onion, finely chopped
1/2 cup finely chopped fresh parsley
1 tablespoon minced garlic
3 tablespoons vegetable oil
4 boneless skinless duck breasts
1/2 teaspoon salt
1 cup seasoned bread crumbs
3 eggs
1/2 cup milk
Vegetable oil for frying

Makes 10 patties

Spread the pecans over a baking sheet. Bake at 350 degrees for 5 to 10 minutes or until toasted. Remove to a shallow dish and let cool.

Sauté the white onion, green onion, parsley and garlic in 3 tablespoons oil until the vegetables are tender. Remove from the heat and let cool.

Grind the duck in a food processor to the consistency of sausage. Remove to a bowl. Add the onion mixture, salt and bread crumbs and mix well. Shape into 2-inch patties, 1/2-inch thick.

Beat the eggs and milk in a bowl. Dip the duck patties in the egg mixture and coat in the pecans. Repeat if a thicker crust is desired.

Heat oil to 350 degrees in a deep skillet. Add the patties and fry until golden brown on both sides and cooked through. Remove to paper towels to drain. Serve with rice and gravy.

 Neal Sinclair

POMEGRANATE HONEY-GLAZED DUCK BREAST WITH PISTACHIO CRUST

1 cup pomegranate juice
1/2 cup honey
1/2 teaspoon ground coriander
1/2 teaspoon cinnamon
1/2 teaspoon ground allspice
1/4 teaspoon cayenne pepper
(or to taste)
6 garlic cloves, crushed
4 boneless mallard breasts
2 teaspoons kosher salt
1/4 cup pistachios, finely chopped
1/3 cup pomegranate-flavored vodka
(optional)
Hot roasted spaghetti squash

Serves 4

Combine the pomegranate juice, honey, coriander, cinnamon, allspice, cayenne pepper and garlic in a bowl and mix well. Add the duck and turn to coat, Marinate, covered, in the refrigerator overnight, turning occasionally. Remove the duck and pour the marinade into a saucepan. Bring to a boil and simmer for 10 minutes. Remove from the heat.

Sprinkle the duck with the salt. Heat a skillet over medium-high heat until hot. Add the duck skin side down and cook until the fat is rendered and the skin is browned and slightly crisp. Turn the duck and cook until the duck is cooked through. Remove the duck to a platter and brush with some of the cooked marinade. Sprinkle with the pistachios and keep warm.

Drain the drippings from the skillet and heat the skillet over medium-high heat. Add the vodka and tilt the pan to swirl the vodka. Cook until the vodka is reduced by half. Stir in the remaining marinade and cook until heated through, stirring constantly.

Serve the duck over a bed of roasted spaghetti squash and drizzle with the sauce. Garnish with pomegranate seeds.

Note: To make 1 cup of pomegranate juice, purée 1 1/2 to 2 cups pomegranate seeds in a blender. Strain through a cheesecloth-lined wire mesh strainer into a bowl.

 Hal Brown

There are more than fifty-two species of ducks common to North America.

ROASTED DUCK BREAST WITH BLACKBERRY PORT SAUCE

2 boneless mallard breasts, or
1 boneless goose breast
1/4 cup dry red wine
1/4 cup ruby port
2 tablespoons blackberry jam
1 tablespoons cornstarch
1 tablespoon cold water or wine

Serves 2 to 4

Heat a nonstick ovenproof skillet over medium heat. Add the duck. Cook for 2 minutes or until golden brown on both sides.

Bake the duck in the skillet at 350 degrees for 10 minutes. Turn the duck and bake for 10 minutes longer or until cooked through. Remove the duck to a cutting board and cover with foil to keep warm.

Pour the red wine into the skillet. Cook, stirring constantly and scraping up any browned bits from the bottom of the pan. Stir in the port and jam and bring to a boil.

Dissolve the cornstarch in the water in a small bowl. Stir into the skillet. Cook until the sauce is thickened, stirring constantly. Slice the duck diagonally and serve topped with the sauce.

 Donald Case

DUCK SCALOPPINE WITH DRIED CRANBERRIES

2 tablespoons butter
1 onion, thinly sliced
Salt and freshly ground pepper
to taste
4 boneless skinless duck breasts, cut
into 8 equal pieces (1 1/2 pounds)
1/2 cup instant flour or
all-purpose flour
2 tablespoons butter
1/4 cup olive oil
1/2 cup dried cranberries
3/4 cup dry red wine
1/2 cup chicken stock
1 tablespoon butter

Serves 4

Melt 2 tablespoons butter in an 8-inch skillet. Stir in the onion, salt and pepper. Cook over low heat for 12 to 15 minutes or until the onion is caramelized. Remove from the heat and keep warm.

Pound the duck with a meat mallet between sheets of plastic wrap to 1/4 inch thick. Remove the plastic wrap and season the duck with salt and pepper. Sprinkle the flour over both sides of the duck.

Heat 2 tablespoons butter and the olive oil in a large skillet until hot. Add the duck and cook until well browned on one side. Turn the duck and stir in the cranberries, wine and stock. Cook for 7 to 8 minutes or until the sauce is reduced by one-half and the duck is cooked through. Add 1 tablespoon butter and swirl the pan until the butter is melted. Adjust the seasonings to taste. Serve topped with the caramelized onion.

 Lenny Maiorano

DUCK SIMPLETON

1 tablespoon butter
1 tablespoon olive oil
2 boneless skinless duck breasts, cut into strips, or 1 boneless skinless goose breast, cut into strips
1 tablespoon butter
1 teaspoon olive oil
1/2 cup fresh mushrooms or drained canned mushrooms
1/2 cup chopped onion
1/2 teaspoon thyme
1 garlic clove, chopped
2 tablespoons Southern Comfort or Jack Daniel's®
Salt and pepper to taste
1 package refrigerator bread dough
Crumbled blue cheese or goat cheese (optional)

Serves 8

Heat 1 tablespoon butter and 1 tablespoon olive oil in a skillet. Add the duck and sauté for 3 minutes or to medium-rare. Remove to a bowl.

Add 1 tablespoon butter and 1 teaspoon olive oil to the skillet. Add the mushrooms and onion and sauté for a few minutes. Add the thyme and garlic and sauté until the vegetables are tender.

Add the whiskey and cook for 1 minute. Remove from the heat. Ignite the whiskey with a long match and carefully shake the pan until the flames subside. Add the onion mixture, salt and pepper to the duck and mix well.

Roll out the bread dough to a rectangle on a nonstick baking sheet. Spoon the duck mixture evenly over half the dough. Sprinkle with cheese if using Jack Daniel's® in the recipe. Fold the dough over the filling and pinch the edges to seal.

Bake at 375 degrees for 10 to 15 minutes or until golden brown. Cut into slices and serve.

 Edward Middleton

*T*his is an easy field version of Duck Wellington that can be made with common kitchen ingredients and tastes really great. The Southern Comfort version has a sweet taste and the Jack Daniel's version is suited to adding cheese.

Ducks Unlimited® is the *only* waterfowl conservation organization with a Washington, D.C., staff whose purpose is to work with lawmakers to see that waterfowl needs are represented when congressional issues will have an impact on waterfowl habitat.

Waterfowl Winners

ASIAN MARINATED BLUEBILL STIR-FRY

1/2 cup low-sodium soy sauce
1/3 cup rice vinegar
1/3 cup plum preserves
3 garlic cloves, minced
2 tablespoons sriracha or
Asian chile garlic sauce
1/2 teaspoon freshly ground
black pepper
1/4 cup olive oil
8 bluebills, breasts only,
skin removed
1 tablespoon cornstarch mixed with
equal part cold water
1 red bell pepper, thinly sliced
1 green bell pepper, thinly sliced
1 1/2 cups snow peas, strings removed
2 fresh plums, seeded and diced
4 cups steamed rice
6 green onions, sliced

Serves 4

In a bowl, whisk together soy sauce and next 5 ingredients. While whisking, add 2 tablespoons of the oil in a thin stream until emulsified. Divide mixture in half.

Place bluebill breasts in a nonreactive container and pour half of marinade mixture over the top. Cover and refrigerate for 2 to 4 hours, turning occasionally. Remove from marinade. Discard marinade. Whisk cornstarch mixture into reserved marinade.

Heat remaining 2 tablespoons oil in a large skillet or wok over high heat. Add duck breasts and stir-fry for 2 minutes. Add peppers and cook for 2 minutes. Add snow peas, plums and reserved sauce and bring to a boil. Remove duck and arrange over warm mounded rice. Continue heating sauce until thickened. Stir in green onions and spoon sauce mixture over duck.

Note: Try serving with a wild rice blend.

SFL

This recipe combines sweet plum flavors with Asian spice.

WILD DUCK BREASTS IN CHERRY SALSA

Cherry Salsa
1 tablespoon olive oil
2 tablespoons finely chopped onion
1 jalapeño chile, minced
1/3 cup dried cherries
2 large Italian plum tomatoes,
finely chopped
1/2 teaspoon sugar
1 tablespoon balsamic vinegar
1/4 teaspoon Creole seasoning

Duck
2 boneless skinless mallard or other
puddle duck breasts
1/2 teaspoon Creole seasoning
1/4 teaspoon pepper
1 teaspoon canola oil
1/4 cup red wine
2 tablespoons balsamic vinegar

Serves 2

The Salsa: Heat the olive oil in a skillet over medium heat until hot. Add the onion and jalapeño chile and sauté for 1 minute. Add the cherries and sauté for 2 to 3 minutes. Stir in the tomatoes, sugar, vinegar and Creole seasoning and cook for 3 minutes, stirring constantly. Remove from the heat and keep warm.

The Duck: Season both sides of the duck breasts with the Creole seasoning and pepper. Heat a heavy skillet over medium-high heat for 1 minute. Add the canola oil and heat until hot. Add the duck and reduce the heat to medium. Cook the duck for 5 minutes. Turn the duck and cook for 4 to 5 minutes or until cooked through. Remove the duck to a cutting board and cover to keep warm.

Add the wine and vinegar to the skillet and cook over high heat for 1 minute, stirring constantly and scraping up any browned bits from the bottom of the pan.

Slice the duck on the diagonal. Arrange one duck breast in a fan shape on each serving plate and spoon the pan sauce over the top. Serve the salsa on the side.

Note: Remove the seeds and ribs from the jalapeño chile before chopping if you would like a milder salsa

 Gary Mergl

Birds use more energy when flying very slow or very fast,
so they fly at medium speeds.

TROPICAL DUCK WITH WILD RICE   *Fifth-Place Winner*

3 or 4 mallard or other puddle
duck breasts
6 ounces frozen orange juice
concentrate, thawed
$1/2$ cup water
$1/2$ teaspoon nutmeg
2 (6-ounce) packages dried mixed
tropical fruit
$1^1/2$ cups spiced rum
$1/2$ teaspoon nutmeg
$1/4$ cup olive oil
$1/2$ cup slivered almonds
Hot cooked wild rice

Serves 4

Place the duck in a sealable plastic bag. Mix the orange juice, water and $1/2$ teaspoon nutmeg in a bowl and pour over the duck. Seal the bag tightly and turn to coat. Marinate in the refrigerator for 6 hours to overnight. Remove the duck and pat dry with paper towels. Discard the marinade.

Grill the duck over medium-hot heat until cooked through. Remove the duck to a cutting board and cut into bite-size pieces.

Mix the fruit, rum and $1/2$ teaspoon nutmeg in a saucepan. Simmer for 5 to 10 minutes or until the fruit is plump and the liquid is reduced, stirring occasionally. Stir in the duck, olive oil and almonds. Cook over medium heat until heated through, stirring constantly. Serve over wild rice.

 Kathleen Knapp

BIG T'S YUMMY DUCK AND RICE

2 large ducks, or 3 or 4 small ducks
4 cups chicken stock
2 ribs celery, chopped
1 onion, chopped
1 bell pepper, chopped
3 tablespoons bacon drippings
2 cups brown rice
1/4 cup (1/2 stick) butter
1/2 teaspoon ground cumin
1/4 teaspoon oregano
2 tablespoons Worcestershire sauce
1 teaspoon Louisiana-style hot sauce
1 small jar diced pimentos
1 small can chopped black olives
1/2 teaspoon seasoned salt
1/4 teaspoon pepper

Serves 6 to 8

Add the ducks to the stock in a large saucepan and bring to a boil. Reduce the heat and simmer for 1 hour or until the duck is cooked through.

Remove the ducks to a cutting board and let cool, reserving the stock. Cut the duck meat into 1/2-inch pieces, discarding the skin and bones. Return the duck meat to the stock.

Sauté the celery, onion and bell pepper in the bacon drippings in a skillet for 5 minutes. Add to the stock.

Stir in the rice, butter, cumin, oregano, Worcestershire sauce, hot sauce, pimentos, olives, seasoned salt and pepper. Bring to a boil and then reduce the heat. Simmer, covered, for 25 to 30 minutes or until the rice is tender.

 T. Sims

WOODIE WRAPS

10 boneless wood duck breasts or
any medium to large duck breasts
3 cups milk
4 ounces hot bulk pork sausage
5 ounces cream cheese, softened
5 jalapeño chiles, halved lengthwise
and seeds removed
10 slices bacon
1 1/2 cups honey

Serves 10

Soak the duck breasts cold in water for 2 hours, changing the water every 30 minutes; drain. Marinate in the milk in the refrigerator overnight. Drain and discard the milk.

Pat the duck dry with paper towels. Brown the sausage in a skillet, stirring until crumbly; drain. Remove the sausage to a bowl. Stir in the cream cheese.

Fill the chiles with equal portions of the sausage mixture. Cut a 2-inch slit in each duck breast to form a pocket. Insert 1 stuffed chile filling side down into each pocket and fold the duck meat over the chile. Wrap 1 bacon slice around each duck breast and secure the bacon with a wooden pick. Coat the duck with the honey. Preheat the grill to 400 degrees.

Cook the duck over indirect heat for 20 minutes or until cooked through, brushing occasionally with the honey.

 John Ellen

TEAL IN COGNAC PEAR SAUCE

Teal
2 lean teal, halved
White wine
Garlic cloves, cut in half
Salt and pepper to taste
Butter and grapeseed oil for searing

Cognac Pear Sauce
1/2 cup cremini or button mushrooms
1/4 cup chopped shallots
Butter
1/3 cup chopped peeled pear
1/2 cup cognac
1/3 cup chicken stock
1 teaspoon minced fresh rosemary
1/2 slice bacon, crisp-cooked
and crumbled

Serves 2

The Teal: Marinate the teal in wine in a bowl for 5 minutes. Drain and pat dry with paper towels. Rub the teal with garlic, salt and pepper. Heat a small amount of butter and grapeseed oil in a skillet. Add the teal skin side down and cook for 2 to 3 minutes per side. Remove the teal to a baking pan. Bake until the teal is cooked through.

The Sauce: Sauté the mushrooms and shallots in a small amount of butter in a saucepan until tender. Stir in the pear and cognac. Cook until reduced. Stir in the stock and simmer for 2 to 3 minutes. Stir in the rosemary and bacon and cook until heated through. Pour over the duck in serving bowls. Serve with garlic toast and plenty of napkins.

 Forrest Messerschmidt

BONELESS GOOSE ROAST

1 onion, finely chopped
2 tablespoons butter
12 ounces ground pork or veal
4 ounces cooked ham, shredded
3/4 cup bread crumbs
1 teaspoon chopped parsley
1 teaspoon sage
1/4 cup sherry or white wine
1 egg, beaten
Salt and pepper to taste
1 (4- to 5-pound) Canada
goose, deboned
2 tablespoons olive oil

Serves 6 to 8

Sauté the onion in the butter in a skillet until tender. Add the pork and cook until crumbly; remove to a bowl. Mix in the next 6 ingredient. Season with salt and pepper.

Lay the goose skin side down on a work surface. Spread the stuffing evenly over the goose. Roll up the goose and tie with kitchen twine at 2-inch intervals. Heat the olive oil in a roasting pan in the oven. Place the goose on a rack in the roasting pan and baste with the hot olive oil. Roast at 350 degrees for 1 1/4 to 1 1/2 hours or until the goose is cooked through, basting with the pan drippings every 20 minutes and turning once. Cut into 1/2- to 1-inch slices and serve.

Note: The pan drippings can be used to make gravy.

 Mike Bodensteiner

CANADA GOOSE STIR-FRY

4 boneless skinless goose breasts, cut into bite-size pieces
2 cups cola
1/2 cup soy sauce
Peanut oil
Olive oil
Teriyaki sauce
1 1/2 cups chopped broccoli
1 1/2 cups chopped green, red and yellow bell peppers
1 cup snow peas
1/2 cup chopped sweet onion
1/2 cup baby corn
1 (8-ounce) can water chestnuts, drained
Hot cooked white rice

Serves 4 to 6

Combine the goose, cola and soy sauce in a bowl and mix well. Marinate in the refrigerator overnight. Drain and discard the marinade.

Add equal portions of peanut oil and olive oil to a large cast-iron skillet and heat until hot. Add the goose and sauté until the goose is cooked through. Remove the goose to a bowl. Rinse the skillet and return to the heat.

Add equal portions of the peanut oil and olive oil to the skillet along with a splash of teriyaki sauce and heat until hot. Add the broccoli, bell peppers, snow peas, onion, baby corn and water chestnuts carefully and cook, covered, until the vegetables are tender-crisp, stirring frequently. Stir in the goose and cook until heated through. Serve over white rice.

 Christopher Schott

SNOW GOOSE FRICASSEE

1/4 cup (1/2 stick) butter
4 boneless skinless snow goose breasts
3 Granny Smith apples, peeled and cut into 1/4-inch slices
1/2 cup packed light brown sugar
1/2 teaspoon cinnamon
1/2 cup dry white wine

Serves 4

Melt the butter in a large skillet over medium-high heat. Add the goose and sear on both sides. Remove the goose to a cutting board and cut into 1/4-inch slices.

Return the goose to the skillet. Add the apples, brown sugar and cinnamon. Sauté over medium heat until the apples are tender and the goose is cooked through. Add the wine and sauté over medium-high heat for 1 minute. Serve with rice.

 Dawn Webb

ESPRESSO GOOSE

1 garlic bulb
1 fennel bulb, cut into chunks
3 ribs celery, cut into chunks
2 onions, cut into chunks
Vegetable oil
4 goose fillets
2 tablespoons instant
espresso powder
1 cup Hunan hot duck sauce
1 cup white wine
1 can beef broth
1 cup water
6 slices bacon, chopped
1 small jar sun-dried tomatoes
Rosemary to taste
2 tablespoons balsamic vinegar
(or to taste)

Serves 4

Cut off the top of the garlic bulb. Toss the fennel, celery and onions with a small amount of oil in a bowl to coat. Spread the vegetables in a roasting pan and add the garlic, cut side up. Bake at 350 degrees for 45 minutes.

Remove the fennel, celery and onions to a large saucepan and squeeze the garlic from the cloves into the saucepan. Add the goose, espresso powder, duck sauce, wine, broth, water, bacon, tomatoes and rosemary and mix well. Simmer for 2 1/2 hours or until the duck is cooked through. Stir in the vinegar.

 Alfred Ingulli

GOOSE ENCHILADA ROLL-UPS

4 boneless skinless goose breasts
4 ounces whole green chiles
1/2 cup (2 ounces) shredded
Monterey Jack cheese
4 teaspoons chopped black olives
1 egg
1 cup crushed tortilla chips
1/4 cup vegetable oil
1 envelope enchilada seasoning mix
1/2 cup water
1 (16-ounce) can diced tomatoes
1/2 cup (2 ounces) shredded
Cheddar cheese

Serves 4

Pound the goose breasts on a work surface with a meat mallet to flatten. Spread equal portions of the chiles, Monterey Jack cheese and olives over each goose breast. Roll up and secure with wooden picks.

Beat the egg in a bowl. Dip the roll-ups in the egg and coat in the tortilla chips. Heat the oil in a skillet. Add the roll-ups and fry until golden brown on all sides. Remove to a baking dish.

Mix the seasoning mix, water and tomatoes in a saucepan. Cook for 15 minutes, stirring occasionally. Pour over the roll-ups. Bake at 350 degrees for 35 minutes or until the goose is cooked through. Sprinkle with the Cheddar cheese and bake 5 minutes longer.

 Keith Frey

James's Glazed Wild Goose Breasts

4 goose breasts
Splash of vermouth (optional)
Salt to taste
1 tablespoon grated orange zest
Juice of 1 orange
1 teaspoon lemon juice
1 teaspoon brown sugar
1 garlic clove, minced
1 tablespoon soy sauce
1/2 teaspoon dry mustard
1/4 teaspoon caraway seeds

Serves 4

Arrange the goose breasts in a baking dish. Splash with the vermouth and sprinkle with salt. Whisk the orange zest, orange juice, lemon juice, brown sugar, garlic, soy sauce, dry mustard and caraway seeds in a bowl. Pour evenly over the goose.

Bake at 350 degrees for 30 minutes or until the goose is cooked through, basting at least twice with the cooking liquid.

 James Clements

Marais des Cygne Roast Goose

Goose
1 wild Canada goose, dressed
1 orange, cut into wedges
8 dried apricots or prunes, chopped
1 apple, cut into wedges
8 juniper berries, crushed (optional)
1 envelope onion soup mix
1 can beef consommé
1 cup water
1 cup marsala

Red Currant Sauce
1/2 cup red currant jelly
1/3 cup ketchup
1/4 cup Worcestershire sauce
1/2 cup marsala or port
3 tablespoons butter or margarine

Serves 6

The Goose: Stuff the goose cavity with the orange, apricots, apple and juniper berries. Place the goose breast side up in a plastic cooking bag. Combine the soup mix, consommé, water and wine in a bowl and mix well. Pour over the goose and seal the bag using the package directions. Place in a shallow roasting pan and cut a few small slits in the top of the bag.

Bake at 350 degrees for 2 1/2 hours or until the goose is cooked through. Remove the goose to a cutting board and tent with foil to keep warm.

The Sauce: Combine the jelly, ketchup, Worcestershire sauce, wine and butter in a saucepan. Cook over medium heat until hot, stirring frequently. Slice the goose and arrange on serving plates. Drizzle with the sauce and serve with garlic mashed potatoes.

 Bill McKee

WILD GOOSE OR DUCK IN PLUM SAUCE

Goose

3 or 4 boneless skinless
goose breasts, or 6 to 8 boneless
skinless duck breasts
1/2 cup soy sauce
1/2 cup sugar
Pinch of salt
Pinch of pepper
All-purpose flour
Vegetable oil

Plum Sauce

2 tablespoons sugar
1 1/4 teaspoons salt
1/2 cup plum sauce
3 tablespoons dark soy sauce
1 teaspoon garlic powder
2 tablespoons frozen orange juice
concentrate, thawed
1/4 cup sherry
1 1/2 cups water
1 onion, chopped
Cornstarch
Hot cooked rice, couscous or quinoa

Serves 6 to 8

The Goose: Cut the goose into 1/4-inch strips and place in a bowl. Add the soy sauce, sugar, salt, pepper and enough water to cover and mix well. Marinate in the refrigerator for several hours to overnight. Drain and discard the marinade.

Coat the goose strips in flour. Heat a small amount of oil in a large heavy saucepan. Add the goose and cook until browned on all sides.

The Sauce: Combine the sugar, salt, plum sauce, soy sauce, garlic powder, orange juice, sherry, water and onion in a bowl and mix well. Pour over the goose in the saucepan. Simmer, covered, for 1 hour or until the duck is cooked through.

Dissolve a small amount of cornstarch in a small amount of water in a bowl and add to the goose mixture. Cook until thickened, stirring frequently. Serve over rice, couscous or quinoa.

 Daniel Rice

The relative age of a duck or goose can be determined by looking at the bird's tail feathers. Notches at the end of the feather indicate a juvenile bird.

 *Main Dishes*

Sunset Refuge *(1992)*

Michael Sieve

International Artist of the Year
—1992

Michael Sieve is a Minnesota wildlife artist known as the mammal artist whose collectable works include caribou, moose, song birds, waterfowl, and wild turkey. In a ten-year period, Sieve produced thirty-eight oil paintings that were reproduced as limited editions, twenty-one of which have sold out.

The artist's studio overlooks twenty-five acres of farm land, part of which he has turned into a wildlife preserve. Here, he captures animals in all their moods and motions. Sieve's artworks have landed him many awards, including the First of State in Oregon's Duck Stamp contest from 1984 through 1986. Additionally, Sieve has been recognized by The Minnesota Deer Hunters and the Minnesota Conservation Federation with limited-edition print programs. He also captured the Artist of the Year for the Iowa Bowhunters award in 1983 and was named 1992 Artist of the Year for Ducks Unlimited®.

MICHAEL SIEVE
©-1991

GRILLED HOISIN DUCK BREAST APPETIZERS

3 pounds (or less) boneless skinless
duck breasts and tenders
1 (20-ounce) bottle hoisin sauce
1/4 cup sambal oelek
1 cup dry red wine
1 bunch green onions, chopped
1/4 cup finely chopped fresh ginger
1/4 cup finely chopped garlic
3 tablespoons canola oil

Serves 10 to 12

Cover the duck with plastic wrap on a cutting board and pound with a meat mallet to uniform thickness. Remove the plastic wrap and cut the duck into 1-inch strips. Combine the hoisin sauce, sambal oelek, wine, green onions, ginger, garlic and canola oil in a glass bowl or stainless steel bowl and mix well. Remove and reserve 3/4 to 1 cup of the marinade.

Add the duck to the remaining marinade and stir to coat. Marinate in the refrigerator for 4 to 24 hours. Drain and discard the marinade. Soak bamboo skewers in water for 20 minutes; drain. Thread each duck strip onto a skewer. Preheat the grill to medium-high heat and coat the cooking rack with nonstick cooking spray. Grill for 5 to 8 minutes for medium-rare, turning once or twice to avoid burning.

Arrange the skewers on a serving platter and garnish with lettuce leaves, shredded carrot and toasted sesame seeds. Serve with the reserved marinade for dipping.

Note: Sambal oelek is a hot chile paste. Hoisin sauce and sambal oelek are available at Asian markets and some supermarkets.

 M. Elizabeth Foster

LUCKY DUCK GRILLIN' MARINADE

2 tablespoons salt
3 cups cold water
6 to 8 boneless skinless duck fillets
1/4 cup soy sauce
1/4 cup canola oil
1/4 cup orange juice
1/2 tablespoon ground ginger
Pinch of cayenne pepper
Drizzle of honey

Makes 10 to 12 appetizer servings

Dissolve the salt in the water in a bowl and add the duck. Soak in the refrigerator overnight; drain. Rinse the duck and pat dry with paper towels.

Mix the soy sauce, canola oil, orange juice, ginger, cayenne pepper and honey in a bowl. Add the duck and turn to coat. Marinate in the refrigerator for 6 to 8 hours, turning occasionally. Drain and discard the marinade.

Grill the duck for 3 to 4 minutes per side over high heat for medium-rare.

Note: This is great as an appetizer, or serve it as a main course with your favorite side dish.

 Drew Gaynor

SIMPLY THE BEST GRILLED DUCK BREAST APPETIZERS

6 boneless skinless duck breasts
1/4 cup A.1. steak sauce
1/4 cup soy sauce
2 tablespoons sugar
1/4 teaspoon rosemary
1/4 teaspoon cayenne pepper
1 teaspoon crushed red pepper
1 cup cola
15 slices bacon, each cut into
5 equal pieces

Serves 18

Cut each duck breast into 12 equal portions and place in a 1-gallon sealable plastic bag. Mix the steak sauce, soy sauce, sugar, rosemary, cayenne pepper, crushed red pepper and cola in a bowl and pour over the duck. Seal the bag tightly and turn to coat. Marinate in the refrigerator for 6 hours to overnight. Drain and discard the marinade.

Wrap one piece of bacon around each piece of duck and skewer with a wooden pick to secure. Preheat the grill to 375 degrees. Grill the duck, covered, for 6 minutes per side or until cooked through.

 Greg Harrow

DUCK RUMAKI ZINGERS

2 boneless skinless ducks, cut into
1- to 1 1/2-inch cubes
1/3 cup soy sauce
1/3 cup sherry
1/4 cup sesame oil
2 tablespoons brown sugar
2 tablespoons finely chopped
fresh ginger
1 teaspoon garlic powder
1 (16-ounce) jar sliced jalapeño
chiles, drained
1 pound bacon, slices cut in half

Serves 10 to 12

Place the duck in a sealable plastic bag. Mix the soy sauce, sherry, sesame oil, brown sugar, ginger and garlic powder in a bowl and pour over the duck. Seal the bag tightly and turn to coat. Marinate in the refrigerator overnight. Drain and discard the marinade.

Place one duck piece and one jalapeño chile slice on the end of each bacon slice half. Roll up and secure with a wooden pick. Grill until the bacon and duck are cooked through.

Note: You may use goose instead of duck.

 Ron Nielsen

During the migration, waterfowl will generally return to the same
nesting and wintering locations each year.

GRILLED DUCK FAJITAS

1½ pounds boneless skinless duck breasts
½ cup fresh lime juice
3 tablespoons finely chopped onion
1 large garlic clove, minced
¼ cup golden tequila or dark rum
3 tablespoons vegetable oil
2 large red bell peppers, cut into strips
1 each large green and yellow bell pepper, cut into strips
6 (10-inch) flour tortillas, warmed

Serves 6

Place the duck in a sealable plastic bag. Mix the lime juice, onion, garlic, tequila and oil in a bowl and pour over the duck. Seal the bag tightly and turn to coat. Marinate in the refrigerator overnight, turning occasionally. Drain and discard the marinade. Preheat the grill to medium heat.

Grill the duck for 12 to 15 minutes for medium-rare, turning once or twice. Grill the bell peppers for 6 to 8 minutes or until tender and slightly blackened, turning once or twice. Remove the duck to a cutting board and slice thinly across the grain. Spoon equal portions of the duck and bell peppers over the tortillas and roll up. Serve garnished with salsa, sour cream, guacamole, sliced green onions and/or shredded cheese.

 James Anderson

GRILLED GOOSE FAJITAS

2 envelopes Southwest marinade mix
4 boneless skinless Canada goose breasts, or 6 boneless skinless snow goose breasts, cut into thin strips
2 large green bell peppers, cut into thin strips
2 large sweet onions, cut into thin strips
2 tablespoons bottled minced garlic
3 tablespoons olive oil
12 large flour tortillas

Serves 6

Prepare the marinade mix using the package directions. Combine with the goose, bell peppers, onions and garlic in a large container. Marinate, covered, in the refrigerator for 8 hours, stirring occasionally. Drain and discard the marinade.

Cover the grill cooking rack with foil and pour the olive oil evenly over the foil. Heat the grill to medium-high heat.

Add the goose strips in a single layer on one side of the grill. Add the bell peppers and onions in a single layer on the other side of the grill. Cook for 15 to 30 minutes or until the goose is cooked through and the vegetables are tender-crisp, stirring frequently. Spoon equal portions of the goose and vegetables over the tortillas and roll up. Garnish with salsa, sour cream, shredded cheese and sliced jalapeño chiles. Serve with Spanish rice and refried beans.

Note: I cooked forty geese this way at a goose feed and there was nothing left. Half the people said they didn't like geese; they thought it was beef.

 Susan Passard

BEST GRILLED DUCK SALAD

1/4 cup cranberry juice
1/2 cup orange marmalade
1/2 cup brandy
1 tablespoon soy sauce
1/4 cup white wine
4 boneless puddle duck breasts
1/4 cup white wine vinegar
1/4 cup orange juice
3/4 cup high-quality olive oil
1 tablespoon Dijon mustard
Salt and pepper to taste
4 large handfuls baby field greens
Sliced tomato
Sliced red onion

Serves 4

Mix the cranberry juice, marmalade, brandy, soy sauce and wine in a bowl and pour over the duck in a sealable plastic bag. Seal the bag tightly and turn to coat. Marinate in the refrigerator for several hours to overnight. Drain and reserve the marinade.

Preheat the grill to high heat. Grill the duck for 2 minutes per side for medium-rare. Remove to a cutting board and cover to keep warm.

Cook the reserved marinade in a saucepan over medium-high heat until reduced by two-thirds. Whisk the vinegar, orange juice, olive oil, Dijon mustard, salt and pepper in a large bowl. Add the greens, tomato and onion and toss to mix.

Divide the salad among 4 salad plates. Cut the duck into 1/3-inch slices. Arrange equal portions of the duck over the salads and drizzle with the reduced marinade.

 Bruce Caplin

FLYING PRIME RIB WITH HORSERADISH FOLD

1/2 cup sour cream
1/2 cup mayonnaise
1 tablespoon (or more) grated fresh horseradish
1 cup extra-virgin olive oil
2 tablespoons Worcestershire sauce
2 garlic cloves, crushed
1 tablespoon coarse salt
1 tablespoon coarsely ground pepper
4 small to medium boneless skinless goose breasts

Serves 8

Fold the sour cream, mayonnaise and horseradish together in a bowl until blended. Chill, covered, until ready to serve.

Whisk the olive oil, Worcestershire sauce, garlic, salt and pepper in a large bowl. Add the goose and turn to coat. Marinate, covered, for 2 hours, turning occasionally. Drain and discard the marinade.

Grill the goose over high heat to medium-rare. Remove the goose to a cutting board and let stand for 2 to 4 minutes. Slice the goose across the grain into 1/4- to 1/2-inch slices. Serve with the horseradish sauce on the side.

 Peter Berry

BARBECUED GOOSE STRIPS WITH DIPPING SAUCES

2 (heaping) tablespoons mayonnaise
Juice of 1/2 lemon
4 garlic cloves, crushed and
finely chopped
1 tablespoon chopped cilantro
1/4 cup creamy peanut butter
1/3 cup oil-pack Thai chile paste
1 boneless skinless goose breast
1 (12-ounce) can lemon-lime soda
1/4 cup soy sauce
1/4 cup olive oil
1 tablespoon coarsely ground pepper
(or to taste)
1 teaspoon garlic powder
1/2 head napa cabbage, thinly sliced
Salt to taste

Serves 2 to 4

Combine the mayonnaise, lemon juice and garlic in a small bowl and mix well. Stir in the cilantro. Chill until ready to serve.

Combine the peanut butter and chile paste in a small microwave-safe bowl and mix well. Stir in water if the mixture seems too thick. Microwave on High for 15 seconds and stir.

Cut the goose into 3/4-inch slices. Cut the slices lengthwise into 11/2-inch strips. Combine the goose, soda and soy sauce in a bowl and mix well. Marinate in the refrigerator for 1 to 2 hours. Drain and discard the marinade. Add the olive oil to the goose and mix well.

Soak bamboo skewers in water for 20 minutes; drain. Thread each goose strip onto a skewer and sprinkle with the pepper and garlic powder.

Preheat the grill to high heat and coat the cooking rack with nonstick cooking spray. Grill for 1 to 11/2 minutes per side for medium-rare.

Spread the cabbage over a serving platter and arrange the goose skewers over the cabbage. Season with salt. Warm the peanut butter sauce in the microwave until heated through. Serve the goose skewers with the cold mayonnaise sauce and the hot peanut sauce.

 Marco Stetich

If you want to be fancy, you can serve the goose strips on Asian coleslaw. Add finely sliced carrot, red bell pepper, and green onions to the cabbage in a bowl. Whisk 1/3 cup rice vinegar, 2/3 cup vegetable oil, 1/2 teaspoon sugar, and a dash of salt in a bowl. Pour over the cabbage mixture and toss to mix. Sprinkle with sunflower kernels for extra texture, if desired.

DUCK KABOBS

1/2 cup soy sauce
1/2 cup vegetable oil
1/4 cup sugar
1 teaspoon ginger
2 tablespoons lemon juice
1 tablespoon honey
2 garlic cloves, chopped
4 green onions, chopped
3 jalapeño chiles, chopped
(optional)
8 boneless skinless duck breasts,
cut into 1-inch cubes

Serves 8

Mix the soy sauce, oil, sugar, ginger, lemon juice, honey, garlic, green onions and jalapeño chiles in a bowl. Add the duck and stir to coat. Marinate in the refrigerator for 24 hours or longer. Drain and discard the marinade.

Soak bamboo skewers in water for 20 minutes; drain. Thread the duck cubes onto skewers, leaving a small gap between each cube. Grill over medium heat to medium-rare.

Note: A charcoal grill is recommended since the oil in the marinade may cause problems with a gas grill.

 Adam Ladage

GRILLED GOOSE KABOBS

2 tablespoons lemon juice
1/4 teaspoon Worcestershire sauce
1 tablespoon vegetable oil
1/4 teaspoon liquid smoke
1/4 cup soy sauce
1/4 cup packed brown sugar
1/4 teaspoon grated fresh ginger
4 boneless skinless goose breasts, cut
into 1-inch cubes
4 morels, cut into chunks
2 green, red, yellow and/or orange
bell peppers, cut into chunks
1 can pineapple chunks, drained
2 red onions, cut into chunks
1 package cherry tomatoes

Serves 4 to 6

Combine the lemon juice, Worcestershire sauce, oil, liquid smoke and soy sauce in a bowl and mix well. Stir in the brown sugar and ginger. Add the goose and stir to coat. Marinate, covered, in the refrigerator overnight. Drain and discard the marinade.

Soak bamboo skewers in water for 20 minutes; drain. Thread the goose, mushrooms, bell peppers, pineapple, onions and tomatoes alternately onto the skewers. Grill for 3 to 5 minutes per side or until a meat thermometer inserted into the goose registers 135 degrees.

 Adam Olson

Duck or Goose Roll-Ups

1 cup soy sauce
1 cup granulated sugar
1 cup packed brown sugar
1 cup Worcestershire sauce
3 drops of Tabasco sauce
1/4 teaspoon ground cumin
1/4 teaspoon garlic powder
Salt and pepper to taste
4 boneless skinless duck or goose
breasts, cut into 1/4-inch slices
1 pound maple-cured bacon, slices
cut in half

Serves 6 to 8

Combine the soy sauce, granulated sugar, brown sugar, Worcestershire sauce, Tabasco sauce, cumin, garlic powder, salt and pepper in a bowl and mix well. Add the duck and turn to coat. Marinate in the refrigerator for 4 hours to overnight. Drain and discard the marinade.

Roll up each duck slice and wrap with 1 piece of bacon. Thread onto metal kabob skewers. Grill over medium heat for 1 hour or until the duck is cooked through, turning often. Serve with baked potatoes and grilled Texas toast.

 Mark Dixon

Cliff's Asian Duck Breast

1/4 cup olive oil
1/4 cup soy sauce
2 tablespoons lemon juice
1 tablespoon hoisin sauce
1/2 teaspoon dry mustard
3 or 4 drops of sesame oil
1 garlic clove, crushed
1 tablespoon honey
1 teaspoon crushed red pepper
Breasts of 2 mallards
(or favorite duck)
2 tablespoons hoisin sauce

Serves 4

Whisk the olive oil, soy sauce, lemon juice, 1 tablespoon hoisin sauce, the dry mustard, sesame oil, garlic, honey and crushed red pepper in a bowl. Add the duck and turn to coat. Marinate in the refrigerator for 6 hours. Drain and reserve the marinade.

Brush the duck with 2 tablespoons hoisin sauce. Grill the duck until cooked through. Boil the reserved marinade in a saucepan for 5 minutes and serve as a dipping sauce.

 Cliff Russell

APPLE-STUFFED DUCK

2 boneless duck breasts
4 cups draft cider beer
1 teaspoon garlic salt
1 large Granny Smith apple, cut into 1/4- to 1/2-inch pieces
2 small navel oranges, cut into 1/4- to 1/2-inch pieces
2 tablespoons pine nuts
4 thin-cut slices bacon

Serves 4

Butterfly each duck breast by cutting horizontally to 1/2-inch from the edge and lay open. Arrange the duck in a single layer in a large container. Pour 3 cups of the beer over the duck and sprinkle with the garlic salt. Marinate in the refrigerator for 8 hours to overnight. Drain and discard the marinade.

Lay the duck flat on a work surface. Combine the apple, oranges and pine nuts in a bowl and mix well. Spoon equal portions of the fruit mixture over the center of each breast. Roll up the duck and secure with wooden picks. Wrap each rolled breast with 2 bacon slices. Secure with wooden picks.

Grill over low heat for 15 to 18 minutes or until the duck is cooked through, turning occasionally and basting with the remaining 1 cup beer.

 James Mülle

MARINATED GREATER CANADA GOOSE ON THE BARBIE

1 (10- to 13-pound) Canada goose
2 (12-ounce) cans high-quality root beer
2 cups soy sauce
6 garlic cloves, minced
2 tablespoons olive oil

Serves 6

Place the goose in a heavy 2-gallon sealable plastic bag. Mix the root beer, soy sauce and garlic in a bowl and pour over the goose. Seal the bag tightly, extracting as much air as possible, and turn to coat. Marinate in the refrigerator for 24 hours, turning occasionally. Drain and discard the marinade. Coat the goose with the olive oil.

Preheat 30 charcoal briquettes on opposite sides in a 23-inch covered grill and place a drip pan in the center. Place the goose in the center of the cooking rack. Cook, covered, for 30 minutes until a meat thermometer inserted into the thickest portion registers 140 to 150 degrees.

Remove the goose to a shallow pan and tent with foil to keep warm. Carve the goose and serve topped with the pan drippings from carving.

 Buck Keys

JACK DANIEL'S® GRILLED DUCK BREAST

1 tablespoon good-quality
extra-virgin olive oil
1 to 2 teaspoons fresh garlic, minced
1 tablespoon fresh sage,
finely chopped, or ¹/2 tablespoon
dried sage
2 tablespoons fresh Italian flat-leaf
parsley, chopped fine
6 ounces teriyaki sauce
1 tablespoon brown sugar
1 ounce Jack Daniel's® (or just a
splash more for good measure!)
Salt and freshly ground pepper
4 to 6 duck breast halves

Serve 4 to 6

Mix all marinade ingredients together in a medium bowl. Add duck breasts and toss until evenly coated. Cover and place in refrigerator. Let marinate 2 to 4 hours.

Preheat a charcoal grill (you may use a gas grill, but you just don't get that same flavor). When the flame has just died out and the coals are stacked and hot, start placing the duck breasts on the grill. Cook about 2¹/2 to 3 minutes on each side or until rare to medium-rare. Do not overcook! Remove the duck breasts from the grill and let them rest for a minute. Slice on the bias and serve. It will melt in your mouth.

LMF

This is my variation of a recipe that was prepared for me by my friend Doug Carmean at a backyard barbecue years ago. Doug prefers using brandy in this marinade, but I couldn't resist giving it a twist with Jack Daniel's®. This is by far my favorite duck recipe. I can't take the credit for it, but I can pass it along to anyone who wants to impress their guests with a tasty, simple recipe.

GRILLED DUCK OR GOOSE

1 (or more) duck or goose
1 cup (or less) vinegar
Cajun seasoning
Oranges, cut into eighths
Apples, cut into eighths
Onions, cut into eighths
Injector Cajun marinade (optional)
Garlic butter, melted (optional)
Sliced bacon

Serves 2 or more

Cover the duck with water in a large saucepan. Bring to a boil and add the vinegar. Boil for 10 minutes; drain. Rinse the duck, if desired. Season the duck inside and out with Cajun seasoning. Fill the cavity with oranges, apples and onions. Pour the Cajun marinade into a meat injector. Inject the marinade evenly into the duck. Fill the meat injector with garlic butter and inject evenly into the duck, using the same holes. Cover the duck breast with bacon slices and secure with wooden picks.

Preheat charcoal in a grill. Place the duck breast side down on the cooking rack. Grill for 10 minutes. Turn the duck over and grill for 10 minutes. Move the coals to the outside of the grill. Grill for 45 minutes or until the duck is cooked through, turning every 5 to 10 minutes. Serve with brown rice (I like *River Road Cookbook*'s recipe).

 Harry Henson

NUEVO LATINO DUCK WITH CITRUS-CRANBERRY MOJO

3 tablespoons olive oil
2 teaspoons minced garlic
1 jalapeño chile, seeded and minced
2/3 cup jellied cranberry sauce
1 tablespoon honey
1/3 cup fresh orange juice
3 tablespoons fresh lime juice
2 tablespoons chopped cilantro
1 1/2 teaspoons kosher salt
1 teaspoon ground cumin
1 teaspoon ground coriander
4 boneless wild duck breasts
Olive oil

Serves 4

Heat 3 tablespoons olive oil in a saucepan over medium heat. Add the garlic and jalapeño chile and sauté just until tender. Stir in the cranberry sauce, honey, orange juice and lime juice. Cook until slightly reduced, stirring frequently. Stir in the cilantro. Remove from the heat and let cool.

Mix the salt, cumin and coriander together. Rub the duck breasts with olive oil. Rub the spice mixture onto the duck. Grill the duck, skin side down, to medium-rare, basting with half the sauce during the last few minutes of grilling. Remove the duck to a cutting board and slice.

Serve the duck drizzled with the remaining sauce and garnished with chopped cilantro and orange and lime slices.

 Robert Gadsby

DUCK BREAST TENDERS

1 cup soy sauce
1/2 cup Worcestershire sauce
1/4 cup olive oil
1/4 cup whiskey
2 tablespoons white wine
1/2 teaspoon garlic salt
1/4 teaspoon lemon pepper
1/4 teaspoon black pepper
1/8 teaspoon ginger
6 duck breast fillets
1 pound unpeeled shrimp
8 ounces bacon
1 can sweet corn kernels
1 (4-ounce) can mushrooms
Salt and black pepper to taste
Dash of Worcestershire sauce

Serves 6

Combine the soy sauce, 1/2 cup Worcestershire sauce, the olive oil, whiskey, wine, garlic salt, lemon pepper, 1/4 teaspoon black pepper and the ginger in a bowl and mix well. Add the duck and turn to coat. Marinate in the refrigerator for 2 hours. Drain and discard the marinade.

Pound the duck on a work surface with a meat mallet to flatten. Place 3 shrimp in the center of each duck breast and wrap the duck around the shrimp. Wrap bacon around each duck breast and secure with a wooden pick. Grill over medium heat for 5 minutes on each of four sides or until the duck is cooked through. Remove the wooden pick and peel the shrimp. Mix the corn, mushrooms, salt, pepper to taste and a dash of Worcestershire sauce in a saucepan. Bring to a boil. Drain and serve with the duck, shrimp and bacon.

 James Weber

MIKE'S DUCK BREASTS ON RICE

6 boneless skinless duck breasts
2 (12-ounce) cans beer
1 tablespoon garlic powder
1 tablespoon seasoned salt
1 tablespoon basil
1 tablespoon crushed red pepper
1 teaspoon crushed dried
jalapeño chiles
1 package thick-sliced
peppered bacon
1 package long grain wild rice mix
6 large mushrooms, sliced
2 onions, chopped

Serves 6

Soak the duck breasts in a bowl of salted water; drain. Score the duck with a small sharp knife. Pour the beer over the duck in a bowl. Marinate in the refrigerator for 6 to 12 hours. Drain and discard the marinade.

Mix the garlic powder, seasoned salt, basil, crushed red pepper and jalapeño chiles in a small bowl. Rub evenly into the duck breasts. Wrap the duck breasts with bacon and secure with wooden picks.

Prepare the rice mix using the package directions, adding the mushrooms and onions while the rice is cooking. Grill the duck until cooked through. Serve the duck over the rice.

Note: Hollandaise sauce with a bit of mustard added makes a nice sauce for this recipe.

 Mike Brouwer

GRILLED MALLARD BREAST WITH CURRANT JELLY SAUCE

Currant Jelly Sauce

6 to 8 tablespoons butter
1 (12-ounce) jar currant jelly
1 tablespoon finely chopped
fresh thyme
1 tablespoon finely chopped
fresh rosemary
1 teaspoon finely chopped
fresh savory

Duck

1 package wild rice mix
1 cup olive oil
3 to 4 tablespoons soy sauce
3 to 4 tablespoons lemon juice
2 large mallard breast fillets
Olive oil
Asparagus spears
Butter
Sea salt

Serves 4

The Sauce: Melt the butter in a saucepan and add the jelly. Cook until smooth, stirring frequently. Stir in the thyme, rosemary and savory. Keep warm until ready to serve.

The Duck: Prepare the wild rice using the package directions, substituting chicken broth for water. Keep warm until ready to serve. Whisk 1 cup olive oil, the soy sauce and lemon juice in a glass bowl. Add the duck and turn to coat. Marinate in the refrigerator for 20 to 30 minutes. Drain and discard the marinade. Pat the duck dry with paper towels.

Heat the grill to medium-high heat and coat the cooking rack with additional olive oil. Grill the duck for 3 to 4 minutes per side for medium-rare. Remove the duck to a cutting board and slice very thin, but do not shave. Cook the asparagus in a small amount of water in a covered skillet for 3 to 4 minutes or until tender-crisp; drain. Add a small amount of butter and sea salt and cook until the butter is melted.

Arrange the duck slices on serving plates. Spoon the rice and asparagus onto the plates. Pour the sauce over the duck.

 Bill Palmer

GRILLED PINEAPPLE GINGER DUCK WITH CILANTRO CREAM

Cilantro Cream

2 tablespoons butter
4 garlic cloves, minced
2 tablespoons finely chopped fresh ginger
1/2 cup chopped cilantro
1/4 cup soy sauce
1/2 cup heavy whipping cream
2 tablespoons pineapple juice

Duck

4 cups pineapple juice
6 garlic cloves, chopped
2 small red chiles, finely chopped
2 cups cilantro, chopped
1 cup packed brown sugar
1 cup soy sauce
1/4 cup chopped fresh ginger
6 to 8 boneless skinless duck breasts
2 tablespoons olive oil
Hot cooked white rice or jasmine rice

Serves 6 to 8

The Cream: Heat the butter in a skillet until sizzling. Add the garlic, ginger and cilantro and sauté for 4 minutes. Stir in the soy sauce and cook for 1 minute. Stir in the cream and cook until slightly thickened, stirring constantly. Remove from the heat and stir in the pineapple juice. Keep warm or chill, covered, for up to 2 days.

The Duck: Combine the pineapple juice, garlic, chiles, cilantro, brown sugar, soy sauce and ginger in a bowl and mix well. Add the duck and turn to coat. Marinate, covered, in the refrigerator for 12 to 24 hours, turning occasionally. Drain and discard the marinade. Pat the duck dry with paper towels. Rub the duck evenly with the olive oil.

Grill the duck over medium-high heat until a meat thermometer inserted into the thickest portion registers 130 degrees. Serve the duck over white rice or jasmine rice. Reheat the sauce, if needed, and spoon over the duck.

 Catherine Wilkinson

Dabbling ducks—like mallards and teal—are mostly vegetarians, but will feed on snails and insects, especially during breeding season when they need additional protein and calcium.

GRILLED MARINATED DUCK BREASTS

2 tablespoons minced shallot
or onion
1/2 cup light soy sauce
1 tablespoon Worcestershire sauce
3/4 cup high-quality extra-virgin
olive oil
1/2 teaspoon minced garlic
1/3 teaspoon ground sage
6 to 10 boneless skinless teal or
wood duck breasts
Salt and pepper to taste
Paprika to taste
1/2 cup light soy sauce (optional)
1/8 teaspoon wasabi paste (optional)

Serves 6 to 10

Whisk the shallot, 1/2 cup soy sauce, the Worcestershire sauce, olive oil, garlic and sage in a large bowl. Add the duck and turn to coat. Marinate in the refrigerator for 4 hours or longer, turning frequently. Drain and discard the marinade. Sprinkle the duck with salt, pepper and paprika.

Grill the duck to medium-rare. Remove to a cutting board and slice the duck thinly. Mix 1/2 cup soy sauce and wasabi in a bowl and serve as a dipping sauce.

 Jeanne Ralstin

BLAKE'S HAWAIIAN DUCK BREAST

2 cups pineapple juice
1 cup soy sauce
1 cup Worcestershire sauce
2 tablespoons minced garlic
1 cup honey
8 boneless skinless duck breasts
8 ounces cream cheese, softened
1 can crushed pineapple, drained
1 pound bacon

Serves 8

Mix the pineapple juice, soy sauce, Worcestershire sauce, garlic and honey in a saucepan. Cook until steaming, stirring frequently. Remove from the heat and let cool. Cut a lengthwise slit in each duck breast to form a pocket. Prick the duck breasts all over with a fork. Place the duck in a sealable plastic bag. Pour the cooled marinade over the duck. Seal the bag tightly and turn to coat. Marinate in the refrigerator for 12 hours or longer. Drain and discard the marinade.

Combine the cream cheese and pineapple in a bowl and mix well. Spoon equal portions of the cream cheese mixture into the duck breast pockets. Wrap each breast with bacon and secure with wooden picks. Grill until the bacon and duck are cooked through.

 Blake Stewart

Honey Chipotle Grilled Duck

2 boneless skinless duck breasts
1/2 cup ketchup
1/4 cup honey
2 tablespoons chopped fresh ginger
2 chipotle chiles packed in adobo sauce
2 tablespoons adobo sauce (from the canned chiles)

Serves 2

Pound the duck breasts on a work surface with a meat mallet to 1/4-inch thick. Place the duck in a shallow dish. Purée the ketchup, honey, ginger, chipotle chiles and adobo sauce in a food processor. Pour evenly over the duck. Marinate in the refrigerator for 2 to 8 hours. Drain and discard the marinade.

Grill the duck for 5 minutes per side or until cooked through. Serve with mashed potatoes.

 Chad Amundson

Marinated Goose Breasts

4 boneless skinless goose breasts
3 tablespoons lemon juice
1 teaspoon brown sugar
1/2 teaspoon salt
1 teaspoon garlic powder
1/2 teaspoon onion powder or dried onion flakes
1/3 cup olive oil
4 jalapeño chiles
4 slices bacon

Serves 4

Place the goose in a sealable plastic bag. Mix the lemon juice, brown sugar, salt, garlic powder, onion powder and olive oil in a bowl and pour over the goose. Seal the bag tightly and turn to coat. Marinate in the refrigerator for 8 hours. Drain and discard the marinade.

Cut a deep lengthwise slit in each goose breast to form a pocket. Insert 1 jalapeño chile into each pocket and fold the goose meat over the chile. Wrap 1 bacon slice around each goose breast and secure the bacon with a wooden pick. Preheat the grill to 400 degrees. Grill the goose breasts for 5 to 8 minutes per side or to medium-rare.

 Richard Eiman

The best ways duck hunters can help guarantee our hunting heritage is by volunteering for their local DU™ committee and making financial contributions to DU™ today. Visit www.ducks.org

MELT-IN-YOUR-MOUTH MALLARD

6 mallard breasts, trimmed
2 cups white wine
1 cup packed brown sugar
1 tablespoon Worcestershire sauce
1 tablespoon balsamic vinegar
1 shallot, minced
4 garlic cloves, crushed
1 sprig of fresh rosemary, minced
1 teaspoon kosher salt
Freshly ground pepper to taste
Salt to taste

Serves 6

Score the duck breasts with a small sharp knife to make a diamond pattern on both sides. Mix the wine, brown sugar, Worcestershire sauce, vinegar, shallot, garlic, rosemary, 1 teaspoon salt and pepper in a bowl. Add the duck and turn to coat. Marinate in the refrigerator for exactly 5 hours. Drain and discard the marinade. Season the duck with salt and pepper to taste.

Preheat the grill at high heat for 10 minutes. Grill the duck for $3^1/_2$ minutes per side for medium. Remove the duck to a cutting board and slice thinly.

 Tom Steffner

ORANGE MARINATED DUCK

2 tablespoons chopped onion
1 teaspoon minced garlic
$^1/_2$ cup olive oil or peanut oil
$^1/_4$ cup orange juice
1 teaspoon salt
1 teaspoon pepper
$^1/_4$ cup packed brown sugar
4 duck breasts

Serves 4

Mix the onion, garlic, olive oil, orange juice, salt, pepper and brown sugar in a bowl. Add the duck and turn to coat. Marinate, covered, in the refrigerator for 2 hours or longer. Drain and discard the marinade. Grill the duck for 5 minutes per side for medium-rare.

 Lucy Lercel

SOUTHWESTERN DUCK WITH CHIPOTLE-APRICOT GLAZE

First-Place Winner

16 cups (1 gallon) water
3 tablespoons finely
chopped cilantro
1/2 cup plus 2 tablespoons salt
1/2 cup honey
1/4 cup packed dark brown sugar
2 teaspoons onion powder
1 teaspoon garlic powder
1 tablespoon mixed pickling spice
4 boneless skinless teal or
wood duck breasts
1 jar apricot jam
1 tablespoon finely chopped seeded
chipotle chile packed in adobo sauce

Serves 4

Mix the water, cilantro, salt, honey, brown sugar, onion powder, garlic powder and pickling spice in a large container. Add the duck breasts. Marinate in the refrigerator for 6 hours to overnight. Drain and discard the marinade. Pat the duck dry with paper towels. Mix the jam and chipotle chile in a saucepan. Simmer for 5 minutes, stirring occasionally. Strain through a wire mesh strainer into a bowl, if desired.

Grill the duck over high heat to medium-rare, moving infrequently so that grill marks form on the duck. Baste the duck lightly with the apricot glaze just before done. Remove the duck to a cutting board and let stand for a few minutes. Slice the duck diagonally and arrange on serving plates. Drizzle with the remaining apricot glaze and garnish with chopped cilantro or scallions. Serve with wild rice or your favorite side dish.

 Joshua Sasser

"Jimmy's Best" Duck Sauce and Marinade

1 cup soy sauce
3/4 cup fresh lemon juice
1/2 cup olive oil
5 garlic cloves, crushed
1 tablespoon hoisin sauce
1 tablespoon ginger
1 teaspoon cayenne pepper
1 teaspoon black pepper
4 or 5 ducks, halved

Serves 8 to 12

Process the soy sauce, lemon juice, olive oil, garlic, hoisin sauce, ginger, cayenne pepper and black pepper in a blender. Pour over the ducks in a large container and turn to coat. Marinate in the refrigerator for up to 6 hours. Drain and reserve the marinade. Boil the reserved marinade in a saucepan for 5 minutes. Grill the ducks to medium-rare. Brush with the reserved marinade and serve.

 Jim Karsant

Rotisserie Roasted Duck

4 cups orange juice
2 cups pineapple juice
1 large duck
1 teaspoon black pepper
1 1/2 teaspoons salt
1 teaspoon rosemary
1 1/2 teaspoons cayenne pepper
1 teaspoon paprika
1 tablespoon chopped garlic
2 tablespoons brown sugar

Serves 4

Mix the orange juice and pineapple juice in a large bowl. Add the duck and turn to coat. Marinate in the refrigerator for 24 hours. Drain and reserve the marinade. Pat the outside of the duck dry with paper towels.

Mix the black pepper, salt, rosemary, cayenne pepper and paprika in a bowl. Rub evenly over the duck. Mix the garlic and brown sugar in a bowl and spoon into the duck cavity. Pour some of the reserved marinade into a meat injector. Inject evenly into the duck, being careful not to inject so much that it runs out and washes off the dry rub. Discard any remaining marinade. Position the duck on a rotisserie, using the manufacturer's directions.

Grill over low heat for 4 1/2 hours or until the outside is very crisp. Remove the duck to a cutting board and let stand for 30 minutes before carving.

Note: You may roast the duck in the oven instead of grilling. Place the duck on a rack in a shallow roasting pan. Roast at 350 degrees for 2 1/2 hours or until the outside is very crisp.

 Mike Egan

GRILLED CORNED BREAST

4 to 6 boneless skinless goose breasts
8 to 12 cups water
1/2 cup canning & pickling salt
1/2 cup Tender Quick salt or
other curing salt
3 tablespoons sugar
2 tablespoons mixed pickling spice
2 bay leaves
8 black peppercorns
2 garlic cloves, minced
Shredded cheese
Chopped jalapeño chiles
Chopped onions
Sliced bacon

Serves 6 to 8

Combine the goose, water, canning salt, Tender Quick salt, sugar, pickling spice, bay leaves, peppercorns and garlic in a large enamel saucepan. Bring just to a boil, stirring frequently. Remove from the heat and let cool. Marinate, covered, in the refrigerator for 4 to 5 days, turning the goose occasionally; drain.

Rinse the goose with cold water. Return the goose to the saucepan and enough cold water to cover. Bring to a boil; drain. Add enough cold water to cover. Bring to a boil; reduce the heat. Simmer, covered, for 3 1/2 to 4 1/2 hours or until tender; drain.

Remove the goose to a cutting board and slice each breast in half horizontally. Layer cheese, jalapeño chiles and onions over half the goose slices and top each with more cheese. Top with the remaining goose slices. Wrap 2 to 4 bacon slices around each breast and secure with a wooden picks. Grill over a low gas flame until the bacon is cooked through.

 Rodd Schulz

North Dakota alone is home to more than a third of the nation's waterfowl production areas.

SMOKED GOOSE APPETIZERS

3 cups water
²/₃ cup packed brown sugar
¹/₃ cup maple syrup
¹/₃ cup corn syrup
¹/₄ cup salt
1 cup soy sauce
1 tablespoon onion powder
1 tablespoon garlic powder
2 tablespoons grated fresh ginger
4 boneless skinless goose breasts
8 ounces cream cheese, softened
1 (14-ounce) can whole
cranberry sauce
Whole wheat crackers

Serves 24 to 32

Combine the water, brown sugar, maple syrup, corn syrup, salt, soy sauce, onion powder, garlic powder and ginger in a bowl and mix well. Add the goose and turn to coat. Marinate in the refrigerator for 12 to 24 hours. Drain and discard the marinade. Pat the goose dry with paper towels.

Combine the cream cheese and cranberry sauce in a bowl and mix well. Chill until ready to serve.

Prepare a smoker with applewood chips using the manufacturer's directions. Add the goose to the smoker and smoke for 2 to 3 hours. Remove the goose to a sheet of foil and wrap the foil around the goose. Bake at 300 degrees for 30 to 45 minutes or until the goose is cooked through. Remove the goose to a cutting board and let cool. Spread equal portions of the cream cheese mixture over the crackers. Slice the goose thinly and top each cracker with a slice of goose.

 Mark Pepin

HAMMER'S SMOKED DUCK STRIPS

2 cups teriyaki sauce
1¹/₂ cups water
¹/₄ cup Sugar Cure or other
curing sugar
¹/₄ cup packed brown sugar
2 tablespoons chopped garlic
packed in water
12 boneless skinless mallard breasts,
cut into ¹/₄-inch strips

Serves 12

Combine the teriyaki sauce, water, Sugar Cure, brown sugar and garlic in a large bowl and stir occasionally for 1 hour or until the sugar is dissolved. Add the duck and stir to coat. Marinate in the refrigerator for 7 days or longer, stirring twice a day. Drain and discard the marinade.

Prepare a smoker with applewood chips using the manufacturer's directions; do not add water to the chips. Add the duck to the smoker. Smoke over low heat for 4 to 5 hours or until the duck is 95% cooked through, adding wood chips and checking the duck every 45 minutes. Remove the duck to a large platter and let cool.

 Scott Hammer

CROSS SMOKED DUCK BREASTS

6 duck breasts
1 (16-ounce) bottle Italian salad dressing
1 tablespoon seasoned salt
6 slices bacon

Serves 4

Skin and debone the duck breasts. Combine the meat with Italian dressing in a bowl. Refrigerate for 4 to 6 hours. Remove the meat from dressing. Sprinkle with the seasoned salt. Wrap with bacon and secure bacon with wooden picks. Grill over a charcoal fire with wet hickory chips added for 18 to 20 minutes, turning twice.

SMOKY MAPLE DUCK OR GOOSE BREAST

1 cup Tender Quick salt or other curing salt
4 cups cold water
3 or 4 boneless skinless duck or goose breasts
1 bottle pure maple syrup
Cajun or Creole seasoning
Brown sugar

Serves 4 to 8

Dissolve the salt in the water in a bowl. Add the duck and turn to coat. Marinate in the refrigerator overnight. Drain and discard the marinade. Rinse the duck with cold water and pat dry with paper towels.

Pour most of the maple syrup into a meat injector. Inject evenly into the duck. Rub the remaining maple syrup over the duck. Mix Cajun seasoning and brown sugar in a bowl. Rub evenly over the duck.

Prepare a smoker using the manufacturer's directions. Add the duck to the smoker and smoke for 2 to 4 hours for duck or 4 to 6 hours for goose or to medium-rare. Remove the duck to a cutting board and slice.

 Lance Lang

Ducks Unlimited® and our conservation partners have conserved more than six million acres of critical waterfowl habitat in the Prairie Pothole Region.

MAPLE-SMOKED DUCK

2 to 4 boneless duck breasts
Worcestershire sauce
Soy sauce
Salt and pepper to taste
1 garlic clove, chopped
1 package maple-flavored bacon

Serves 4 to 6

Butterfly each duck breast by cutting horizontally to $1/2$ inch from the edge and lay open on a work surface. Prick the duck breasts all over with a fork. Drizzle with Worcestershire sauce and soy sauce and sprinkle with salt and pepper. Sprinkle the garlic evenly over the duck and fold the breasts over. Wrap 1 to $1 1/2$ slices of bacon around each duck breast and secure with a wooden pick.

Prepare a charcoal grill with 25 to 30 briquettes. Move the coals to one side of the grill when hot and add 2 chunks of mesquite wood. Place the duck breasts on the cooking rack on the opposite side of the coals. Cook, covered, for 2 to $2 1/2$ hours or until the bacon is cooked through, adding 7 or 8 briquettes to the fire every 30 minutes.

 Doug Stewart

PICO DE PATO

Whole ducks or geese
Saltwater brine
Favorite dry rub
1 (12-ounce) can beer
Serrano chiles

Serves 4 to 6

Cover the duck with brine in a large container. Marinate in the refrigerator overnight. Drain and discard the marinade. Apply dry rub liberally all over the duck. Remove two-thirds of the beer from the can and add serrano chiles to the remaining beer in the can. Position each duck upright over the open beer can.

Prepare a smoker with hickory wood chips using the manufacturer's directions. Add the duck to the smoker and smoke at 225 degrees for 6 to 8 hours. Remove the beer can and seal the duck in foil. Smoke the duck for 1 hour longer. Remove the duck to a cutting board and carve. Serve with pico de gallo, cranberry compote, spicy mustard, sliced melon and crackers.

Note: This makes a great hors d'oeuvre when watching a football game or after duck hunting.

 Howard Sparkman

Game Birds & Wild Turkey

Dove · Pheasant · Quail · Turkey

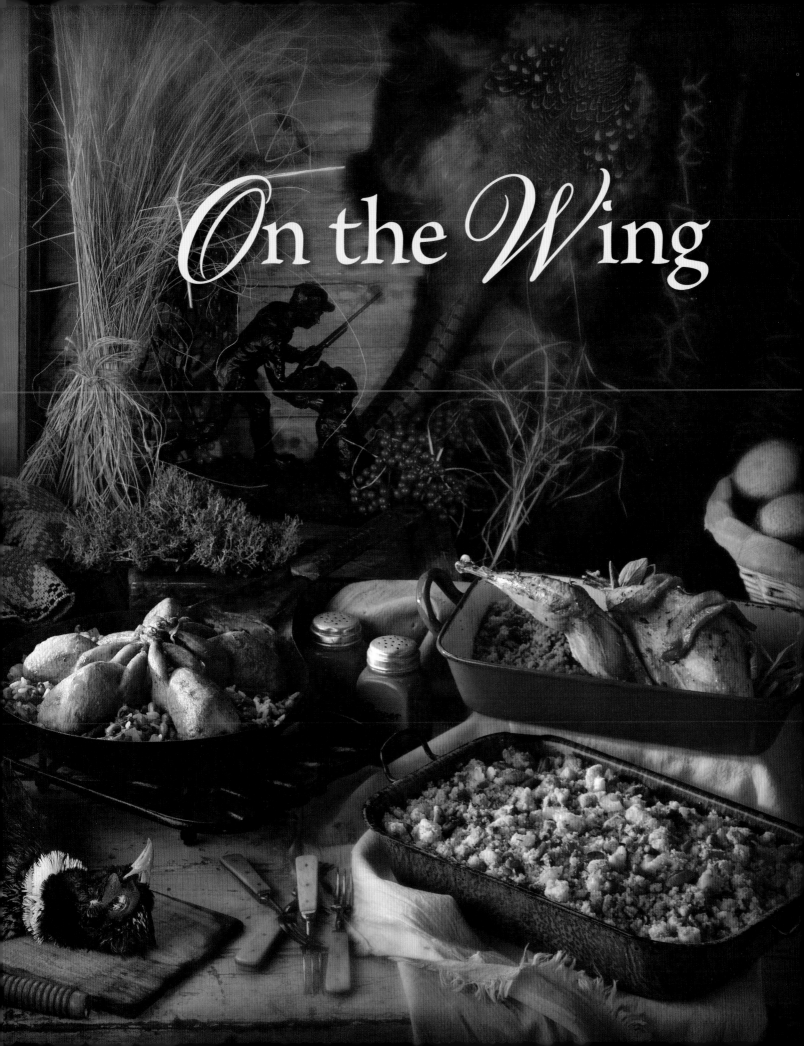

On the Wing

SPICY DOVE ON TOMATO

20 boneless skinless dove
breast halves
2 to 3 tablespoons olive oil
3 tablespoons Cajun seasoning
(store-bought or your own mix)
1 (4-ounce) can diced fire-roasted
chiles (Ortega type)
7 firm tomatoes
1¹/₂ cups (6 ounces) shredded
Monterey Jack cheese

Serves 4 to 6 as appetizers

Toss doves in olive oil and then season liberally with Cajun seasoning. Heat a heavy-duty pan on high heat until very hot. Add dove breasts and cook on each side until well-browned, but not cooked past rare to medium-rare. Remove doves from pan and allow to cool. Slice tomatoes into 20 slices. Place cooked dove on tomato, top with diced chiles and Jack cheese. Place under a preheated broiler until cheese is melted and slightly browned.

SFL

Just this once, I want you to try something a little different. This appetizer preparation is spicy, cool, cheesy, and juicy—all in the same bite. Ideally, the doves should be blackened to medium-rare in a screaming hot cast-iron skillet.

DOVE LETTUCE WRAPS

2 or 3 heads iceberg lettuce
2 tablespoons peanut or vegetable oil
1 teaspoon sesame oil
6 green onions, minced
¹/₂ red bell pepper, finely diced
3 garlic cloves, minced
1 tablespoon fresh ginger, minced
1¹/₂ cups skinless dove breast
fillets, chopped
3 tablespoons soy sauce
2 tablespoons rice vinegar
1¹/₂ cups cooked rice
1 (8-ounce) can water
chestnuts, chopped
1 jar hoisin sauce
Sriracha or other Asian chile sauce

Serves 4 to 6

Remove the stem end of the lettuce head. Carefully peel away individual lettuce leaves, starting at the stem end. You don't need full leaves for wraps, smaller pieces will also work. Trim ragged lettuce edges with kitchen scissors, if desired.

Heat peanut and sesame oil in a large skillet or wok over medium-high heat. Add onions, bell pepper, garlic and ginger. Stir-fry for 2 minutes. Add dove meat and stir-fry for 2 minutes more. Add soy sauce, rice vinegar, cooked rice and water chestnuts. Stir-fry until mixture is warmed throughout. Transfer to a medium bowl.

To serve, place lettuce cups on a plate. Guests make their own lettuce wraps by first spreading a thin layer of hoisin sauce in the center of a lettuce cup. Then add a spoonful or two of the dove mixture and, if desired, a drop or two of the chile sauce.

SFL

On the Wing

DOVE, MANGO AND BACON

1/4 cup olive oil
1 tablespoon sesame oil
1/4 cup soy sauce
1/4 cup rice vinegar
2 tablespoons brown sugar
1 teaspoon freshly ground
black pepper
1 tablespoon Tabasco sauce
16 to 20 boneless dove breasts
1 slightly underripe mango
12 to 15 slices of bacon, cut in half
and partially cooked

Serves 4 to 6 as appetizers

Soak small wooden skewers in water for 30 minutes. Combine olive oil in a bowl with next 6 ingredients. Add dove breasts, cover and marinate for 2 to 3 hours. Remove dove breasts from marinade and pat dry with paper towels. Peel and seed mango and cut into slices. Lay out bacon slices. On each bacon slice lay a slice of mango and a dove breast. Wrap snugly with bacon and secure with small wooden picks. Grill or broil until bacon is done and dove breasts are rare to medium-rare.

SFL

Apparently, there are only two ways to cook doves in the U.S. You can either cook the snot out of them in a tomato or cream sauce or marinate them for an eternity and wrap them in jalapeño and bacon—whatever it takes to make them taste less like doves. I've found that faster is better, as long as you don't cook them too long. This is a variation on the bacon thing.

DOVE AND CREAMY POLENTA

5 tablespoons extra-virgin olive oil
2 pounds cleaned whole doves
Kosher salt and freshly
ground pepper to taste
3 cloves garlic, minced
1 yellow onion, finely diced
1 cup mushrooms, sliced (optional)
1 teaspoon fresh chopped rosemary
1/2 cup fresh Italian flat-leaf parsley,
finely chopped
2 teaspoons fresh thyme, minced
1 cup red wine
16 ounces canned stewed tomatoes
and their juice
1 tablespoon tomato paste
Pinch of crushed red pepper
(optional)
2 tablespoons fresh basil, chopped
4 cups Creamy Polenta (below)
1 cup shredded fontina cheese

Serves 4 to 6

Heat 3 tablespoons of the olive oil in a large stockpot over medium-high heat. Season doves with salt and pepper and sauté until golden brown. Remove doves and set aside.

Return pot to heat and add remaining 2 tablespoons olive oil to the pot. Add onion and sauté for 1 minute. Add mushrooms, rosemary and parsley and sauté for 2 more minutes. Return dove to pot with this mixture; stir.

Add a splash of wine to deglaze the pan and stir with a wooden spoon. Add the stewed tomatoes, 2 cups water, tomato paste, crushed red pepper and the remaining red wine. Stir and reduce heat to a low simmer. Stir occasionally and let simmer for about 2 1/2 hours. Adjust seasonings if needed. Remove from heat and add basil. Serve over Creamy Polenta with shredded fontina melted over the top.

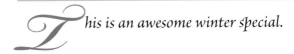

This is an awesome winter special.

CREAMY POLENTA

1/2 cup chicken stock
1/2 cup heavy cream
3 cups water
Pinch of salt
1 cup polenta
1/2 cup shredded fontina cheese

Bring the first 4 ingredients to a boil. Stir in polenta. Reduce heat and cook for about 20 minutes or until creamy. Stir occasionally with a wooden spoon. Stir in 1/2 cup shredded fontina cheese just before removing from heat.

LMF

DOVE KABOBS

1/4 cup Worcestershire sauce
2/3 cup prepared barbecue sauce
1/4 cup olive oil
1 tablespoon dried oregano leaves
3 tablespoons lemon juice
3 garlic cloves, minced
1/2 teaspoon freshly ground
black pepper
1 tablespoon sugar
1/4 cup water
12 to 16 doves, breasts only (will
yield 24 to 32 dove breast halves)
24 small red "creamer" potatoes
2 bell peppers, any color, cut into
1- to 2-inch squares
1 large onion, cut into
1/2-inch pieces
8 medium mushrooms
Olive oil
Salt and pepper to taste

Serves 4

Combine Worcestershire sauce and next 8 ingredients and stir to blend. Place dove breasts in a nonreactive container and pour half the mixture over the top. Toss to coat doves; cover and refrigerate for 2 to 4 hours.

Place potatoes in a microwave-safe bowl with 1/3 cup water. Cover with plastic wrap or paper towel and cook on High for 12 minutes. Place in cold water to cool and then drain thoroughly.

Place peppers, onion, potatoes and mushrooms in a bowl and lightly coat with olive oil, salt and pepper. Alternate pieces of dove, pepper, onion, potato and mushroom on wooden or metal skewers and grill over medium-high heat until doves are rare to medium-rare, about 4 to 5 minutes total cooking time. Serve with reserved marinade for dipping.

S_{FL}

The four flyways—Atlantic, Mississippi, Central, and Pacific—
were first named based on data collected in the 1930s.

Dove Ravioli with Tomato-Basil Vinaigrette

Ravioli

10 to 12 dove breast halves, skin and rib cages removed, seasoned with salt and pepper, broiled until rare and then cooled

1/2 cup Monterey Jack cheese, grated

1/3 cup ricotta cheese

2 garlic cloves, minced

1/4 cup yellow onion, chopped

1 tablespoon dried Italian seasoning

1/4 cup seasoned breadcrumbs

40 won ton wrappers

1/2 cup cornstarch mixed with equal part cold water

Tomato-Basil Vinaigrette

1/4 cup white wine vinegar

1 teaspoon Dijon mustard

1 teaspoon granulated sugar

1/2 cup olive oil

1 cup ripe tomato, chopped

1/4 cup fresh basil, chopped

Salt and pepper to taste

Serves 2 or 3

The Ravioli: Add dove breasts to a food processor and pulse until cut into pea-sized pieces. Add next 6 ingredients and pulse until ingredients are finely minced, but not obliterated.

To make ravioli, place 1 won ton wrapper on a flat surface and spread a thin layer of the cornstarch mixture around the outside edges. Place a small blob of filling in the center of the wrapper, about the diameter of a 50-cent piece and about 1/4 inch high. Place a second won ton wrapper on top of the filling and gently press the edges of the top wrapper onto the moistened edges of the bottom wrapper. Repeat with the remaining ingredients. Place the finished raviolis into a gently boiling pot of lightly salted water. Use plenty of water and don't crowd the pot with too many ravioli at a time. Cook for 3 to 4 minutes or until raviolis are tender and translucent.

The Vinaigrette: Whisk the first 3 ingredients together in a medium bowl. Slowly add oil while whisking. Whisk in tomato and basil and season with salt and pepper. To serve, place 8 to 10 raviolis on a plate and spoon room temperature vinaigrette over.

SFL

*D*on't let the name of this recipe scare you off. It's much easier than it may sound and a great way to stretch your doves if you're a few birds shy of a limit.

DOVE WITH FIGS AND PORT REDUCTION

5 to 7 tablespoons extra-virgin
olive oil
1 1/2 cups fresh or dried figs,
roughly chopped
Pinch of crushed red pepper flakes
Pinch of salt
2 cups port
14 dove breasts, boneless, cleaned,
split and skins removed
Salt and pepper to taste

Serves 4 to 6

Over medium-high heat, warm a medium-large saucepan. Pour in 2 tablespoons olive oil when the pan is hot. Add the figs and quickly sauté for about 2 minutes. Add the red pepper flakes and pinch of salt. Sauté about another minute. Add the port to the pan and reduce the liquid by half. Remove from the heat. Drain port reduction through a fine sieve into a bowl, reserve and set aside.

In a small bowl, drizzle 1 tablespoon olive oil over dove breasts and season lightly with salt and pepper to taste. Heat a medium sauté pan over medium heat. Add the remaining olive oil. When oil appears hot, but not smoking, quickly begin searing dove breasts. You should hear a sizzle when placing doves in pan. (You may need to cook dove in 2 batches). Turn quickly and remove when they are medium-rare. This is a quick process.

Place the dove breasts on a serving platter. Return the sauté pan to heat and pour port reduction into pan to deglaze the seasoning and drippings from the sautéed dove breasts. Reduce for about 2 more minutes or until it has a thick syrup consistency. Pour the port reduction over the dove on the platter and serve.

LMF

PEPPERCORN DOVE BROCHETTE

3 tablespoons whole black
(or other color) peppercorns
1 tablespoon Dijon mustard
1/2 cup dry red wine
1 teaspoon kosher salt
2 garlic cloves, minced
1/4 cup olive oil
12 doves, breasts only
(save bodies for stock)
24 whole button mushrooms
1 red bell pepper, cut into
1-inch squares
1 yellow or green bell pepper, cut
into 1-inch squares
1 large red onion, cut into
1-inch squares

Serves 4

Place peppercorns in a blender with next 4 ingredients and process until pepper is coarsely ground. While motor is running, drizzle oil into mixture in a thin stream. In a large bowl, combine dove breasts with vegetables and toss with peppercorn mixture to coat evenly. Refrigerate for 2 to 6 hours.

Soak 8 large wooden skewers in water for 30 minutes. Alternate dove breast, bell pepper, onion and mushroom on each skewer, with 3 dove breast halves on each skewer. Broil or grill until dove is medium-rare.

Note: You can soak a wooden skewer for 30 days and it will still burn if the grill is hot. I often grill everything off the skewer. To serve, I'll slide the goods onto new skewers for presentation.

SFL

Now that your freezer is loaded with doves, it's time to slap them on the grill while the weather is warm and the doves are not yet freezer burned. No doubt you're aware that freshly ground peppercorns deliver more flavor then the preground stuff. The reason that restaurant servers offer freshly ground pepper is not to fleece you for a few more bucks. It makes the food taste better, and that's nothing to sneeze about.

Since 1973 more than 433,000 guns have been sold through Ducks Unlimited®'s fund-raising event system, bringing in total revenues of nearly $152 million for DU™ conservation programs.

PHEASANT WILD RICE SOUP

1 pheasant
Flour
Oil for frying
1 (12-ounce) bag wild rice
1 onion
3 (15-ounce) cans chicken broth
1 large can cream of chicken soup
1 1/2 cups milk
3 tablespoons cornstarch to thicken
(mix with 1/4 cup water)
Favorite spices to flavor (garlic, basil,
parsley, seasoned salt, pepper)

Serves 8 to 12

Dredge the pheasant in flour and fry in oil until brown. Debone and chop the meat into small pieces. Cook rice as directed on bag. Dice and brown onions in saucepan. When rice is done, combine all ingredients in a large saucepan and let simmer for 1 hour.

 Cheyenne-Ridge Signature Lodge

Cheyenne Ridge Signature Lodge offers exceptional flight wing shooting, premier fishing, and championship golf in the heart of South Dakota pheasant country. Once hunters return from the field, they find that the food prepared by Chef Carl Hawkinson rivals the hunting.

SIGNATURE LODGE PHEASANT CHOWDER

1 medium onion, chopped to
yield 1/2 cup
1/4 cup (1/2 stick) butter
1/4 cup all-purpose flour
1/2 teaspoon seasoned salt
1/4 teaspoon ground pepper
3 cups chicken broth
5 medium cucumbers, peeled and
chopped (about 2 pounds)
2 cups cubed boiled pheasant
1/2 cup long grain rice plus 1/2 cup
wild rice
2 tablespoons lemon juice
2 bay leaves
1 cup light cream
1/4 cup snipped parsley

Serves 6

In 3-quart saucepan, cook onion in butter until tender but not brown. Blend in flour, seasoned salt and ground pepper. Stir in chicken broth. Cook and stir until thickened and bubbly. Add cucumbers; cover and simmer for 10 minutes. Pour half the mixture at a time into blender container. Cover and blend on medium speed for 30 seconds. Return all to saucepan.

Stir in pheasant, uncooked rice, lemon juice and bay leaves. Return to boiling. Reduce heat, cover and simmer for 20 to 25 minutes or until rice is tender. Remove bay leaves. Stir in cream and parsley; heat through. Season to taste. Garnish with fresh parsley. Can be frozen.

 Cheyenne-Ridge Signature Lodge

HERB-ROASTED PHEASANT BREASTS

4 to 6 pheasant breast halves,
skin and bones intact
2 garlic cloves, minced
1 cup chopped assorted fresh herbs
such as basil, sage, rosemary,
oregano, tarragon, parsley, etc.
1/2 cup cooked diced smoky bacon
1 lemon, finely diced
(the whole lemon)
1 teaspoon salt
Pinch of pepper

Serves 4

Using your fingers, start at the neck and carefully separate the skin from the meat. Combine garlic and remaining ingredients and spread a thin layer of the mixture between the skin and the meat of each bird. Place remaining herb mixture on the top of the pheasant breasts. If your pheasant breasts do not have any skin, just put all of the herb mixture on the top of the pheasant breasts. Place on a lightly greased baking dish and bake in a preheated 400-degeree oven for 15 to 18 minutes or just until cooked. Time and temperature will vary according to oven and size of pheasant.

SFL

Perfectly cooked pheasant breasts are just the slightest bit pink in the center when removed from the heat. Because they are so lean, they continue to cook even after you take them out of the pan, oven, or off the grill. If you cook your legs the same way, they will be tough and chewy. But do save the legs since they are great for making stocks. For God's sake, do not put your pheasants in a slow cooker with a can of condensed creamed soup. Yes, I know it tastes good—just like creamed soup. You say your pheasant is dry unless you cook it in the slow cooker? Well, stop cooking it so long. If you don't have any skin on your bird, this recipe will still work.

On the Wing

PHEASANT CONFIT

4 pheasant leg/thigh quarters
2 tablespoons olive oil
Sea salt and freshly ground black pepper to taste
3 tablespoons (about) California extra-virgin olive oil
4 to 6 peeled garlic cloves
1/2 teaspoon crushed red pepper flakes
6 sprigs of fresh thyme
1 cup extra-virgin olive oil

Serves 3 or 4

Preheat oven to 300 degrees. Prepare cleaned pheasant quarters by gently rubbing 2 tablespoons olive oil all over the quarters. Season the pheasant with sea salt and pepper. Set aside on a plate.

Heat 3 tablespoons olive oil in a large sauté pan over medium-high heat. When the pan is hot, but not smoking, place pheasant in pan. You should hear a nice sizzle as soon as the meat hits the pan. Add more oil if necessary. Turn over when golden brown and continue searing. Select a baking pan that will fit the pheasant quarters closely together, but not overlapping. This will prevent wasting olive oil and require less to submerge the meat.

Remove the seared pheasant from the sauté pan and place in the baking pan. Add the garlic, red pepper flakes, thyme and 1 cup olive oil, ensuring all ingredients are submerged by the olive oil. Cover tightly with a lid or aluminum foil. Place in preheated oven and bake for 2 hours. Meat should easily pull away from the bone when done. Cook an additional 30 minutes if necessary. Remove the pheasant from the oven when completed cooking. Remove the meat from the baking pan and set aside to rest for about 3 to 5 minutes. Serve while warm. Adjust seasoning to your desire.

LMF

The traditional recipe of confit requires slow cooking in the meat's own fat. Most of us are familiar with duck confit. Here I put my own twist on pheasant by elevating the flavors of the recipe by roasting in a fragrant, flavorful California olive oil with fresh herbs and garlic. The flavors really round out when the pheasant is seasoned with a great salt and freshly ground pepper. This recipe will literally melt in your mouth!

Savory Herbed Pheasant over Penne Pasta

12 ounces penne
1/4 cup plus 3 tablespoons extra-virgin olive oil
4 boneless, skinless pheasant breasts, cubed
Salt and freshly ground pepper to taste
1/2 teaspoon each ground sage, dried oregano and dried basil
2 garlic cloves, minced
1/2 cup sun-dried tomatoes (packed in oil and drained), julienned
Pinch of crushed red pepper flakes
2 tablespoons balsamic vinegar
Freshly grated Parmigiano-Reggiano cheese

Serves 4 to 6

Prepare the penne using the package directions. Toss with several tablespoons olive oil to coat. Toss pheasant with a bit of olive oil and season with salt and pepper prior to cooking.

Heat a medium-size sauté pan over medium-high heat. Add remaining 1/4 cup olive oil to the pan. Toss in the pheasant breast and sauté quickly; you want some browning/coloration but be careful not to overcook the meat. Add in herbs, garlic, sun-dried tomatoes, pepper flakes and balsamic vinegar. Sauté for about 1 minute. Add to the penne and toss. Finish off by topping with freshly grated cheese.

LMF

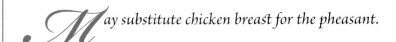

May substitute chicken breast for the pheasant.

Marinated Pheasant Breast with Fresh Garlic and Herbs

3 tablespoons extra-virgin olive oil
2 fresh garlic cloves, minced
1/2 cup fresh parsley, finely chopped
1 tablespoon fresh thyme, minced
1 teaspoon fresh rosemary, minced
Pinch of crushed red pepper (optional)
Salt and freshly ground pepper to taste
4 pheasant breasts (about 6 ounces each) (use more breasts for smaller birds)

Serves 4

In a medium bowl, mix all the ingredients together to completely coat the pheasant breasts. Cover and refrigerate for at least 4 hours.

When ready to prepare, make sure to heat up your cooking source to a good hot temperature. If roasting, place in a preheated 400-degree oven. Or, pan sear over a medium-high heat. Cook pheasant breasts until about 90% cooked through. You do not need to overcook as you would with a chicken breast. Remove from heat and serve.

Note: This goes great with a rice pilaf or over a bed of pasta. If you cook at camp, try it on a crusty French roll for a creative sandwich.

LMF

PHEASANT WRAPPED IN BACON WITH PEPPERCORN SAUCE

4 bacon-wrapped pheasant breasts
2 cups red wine
1 chopped onion
3 garlic cloves, chopped
1 teaspoon tarragon
3 teaspoons green peppercorns
2 cups whipping cream
Rice pilaf

Serves 4

Put the pheasant in a cooking dish and place under the broiler until browned, turning once. Remove from broiler and set on paper towels to drain. Remove excess grease from pan. Deglaze the pan with the wine and pour that into a pot to make the sauce. Add onion, garlic, tarragon and peppercorns. Bring to slow boil. Reduce the mixture by half.

Return the pheasant to the cooking dish. After the sauce is reduced, add the cream. Stir well and pour over the pheasant. Return pheasant to the oven and slow cook at 250 to 300 degrees for 1 to 2 hours. Serve over rice pilaf. Add more cream and wine to increase the amount of sauce, if desired. The green peppercorns may be left whole or crushed. If crushed, the dish tends to be a bit more peppery. Enjoy!

 Cheyenne-Ridge Signature Lodge

PHEASANT AND MANDARIN ORANGE SALAD

8 ounces seasoned and grilled pheasant breasts, diced
1/2 cup mushrooms, sliced
1/2 red onion, sliced
1/2 avocado, diced
1/2 red or yellow bell pepper, diced
1 ripe tomato, diced
1 cup mandarin orange segments
2 tablespoons salted and roasted sunflower seeds
1/4 cup golden raisins
1 tablespoon (approximately) crumbled blue cheese
1 head red leaf lettuce, torn
Freshly ground pepper to taste

Serves 4

In a large salad bowl, toss all ingredients together. Dress with balsamic vinegar and extra-virgin olive oil.

Season with freshly ground pepper. Taste and adjust ingredients to your desire. The blue cheese and balsamic vinegar adds interesting flavor, but make sure your favorite flavors are coming through.

LMF

This is a great dish for a light spring lunch. The pheasant needs to be cooked ahead of time anyway, so why not make it simple and enjoy your guests. Colorful and impressive for something simple!

PHEASANT AND WILD RICE

2 pheasant
All-purpose flour
1 cup wild rice
1 can cream of chicken soup
1 can cream of mushroom soup
1 (8-ounce) can mushroom
stems and pieces
2 1/2 cups water chestnuts (optional)
1 package dry onion soup mix

Serves 6

Debone the pheasant and chop the meat into pieces. Flour and lightly brown pheasant pieces. Mix uncooked rice, canned soups, mushrooms and water chestnuts in baking dish. Add pheasant. Sprinkle dry onion soup mix over top. Cover lightly with foil and bake 1 hour at 300 degrees.

 Cheyenne-Ridge Signature Lodge

PHEASANT TACOS

3 tablespoons vegetable oil
1/2 yellow or white onion, minced
1 1/2 pounds pheasant breasts, cubed
1 jalapeño chile, minced
1/2 cup fresh cilantro, finely chopped
2 teaspoons chili powder
Pinch of dried oregano
Salt and pepper to taste
1/2 cup water
8 corn tortillas

Condiments:
Good-quality salsa
Sliced avocado
Fresh wedges of lemon and limes

Serves 4

Heat the oil in a medium sauté pan over medium-high heat. Add onion and sauté until tender. Add pheasant and jalapeño chile. Sauté for about 10 minutes. Add cilantro and sauté for about 1 more minute. Add chili powder, oregano, salt and pepper. Stir and add about 1/2 cup water. Let cook for about 8 minutes longer. Add more water if needed to prevent drying out.

Remove from heat and serve mixture on fried corn tortillas, or for a lighter version, warm the tortillas in the microwave. Serve with condiments and enjoy!

LMF

This is my favorite rendition of the authentic chicken taco. I love the flavor cilantro adds, but if it is not one of your favorite herbs, feel free to omit it!

As always, I recommend shopping for the best ingredients to complement your meat. Great for a Cinco de Mayo celebration with a frosty margarita!

 On the Wing

SKILLET PHEASANT BREASTS

4 to 6 boneless pheasant breasts,
skin on or off
1/4 cup olive oil
Salt and pepper to taste
2 garlic cloves, minced
3 tablespoons onion, finely diced
2 tablespoons capers
1 teaspoon Dijon mustard
1/4 cup rice vinegar or white
wine vinegar
Pinch of sugar
1/4 cup black olives, chopped
1 cup small tomatoes, quartered
1/4 cup fresh basil or parsley
leaves, chopped
1/3 cup shredded Parmesan cheese

Serves 4

Rub meat with 2 tablespoons olive oil and season with salt and pepper. Heat 1 tablespoon oil in a large skillet over medium-high heat. Add meat and lightly brown on both sides. Add garlic, onion, capers, Dijon mustard, vinegar and sugar. Cook for 2 to 3 minutes. Remove pheasant when just cooked and keep warm. Whisk in remaining 1 tablespoon oil. Add olives, tomatoes and basil and season with salt and pepper to taste. Spoon tomato mixture over cooked pheasant and top with cheese.

SFL

CITRUS QUAIL

Juice of 1 orange (about $3/4$ cup)
Juice of 1 lemon (about $1/4$ cup)
8 whole quail, cleaned and plucked
$1/2$ cup flour
$1/2$ teaspoon salt
$1/4$ teaspoon pepper
5 tablespoons butter
1 teaspoon chicken
bouillon granules
$1/2$ cup hot water
1 unpeeled orange, quartered and
cut into thick slices

Serves 4

Combine the orange juice and lemon juice in a resealable plastic bag. Rinse and dry the quail. Place the birds in the marinade and let sit overnight in the refrigerator.

In a small plastic bag, combine the flour, salt and pepper. Shake the marinade off the birds and then toss them in the flour 2 at a time. Shake off the excess flour. In a 10-inch covered skillet or saucepan, melt the butter just until it starts to sizzle over medium heat. Lightly sauté the quail in the butter until they are golden, about 4 to 5 minutes.

Dissolve the chicken bouillon in the hot water and add it to the pan. Pour in the marinade as well. When the sauce comes back up to a simmer, add the orange slices, cover, and reduce the heat to low. Simmer about 30 minutes or until the quail are tender, basting the birds about every 10 minutes. The sauce will thicken on its own as it cooks. Serve with sliced carrots cooked with a dab of butter.

Note: For the larger, older, and tougher quail in your game vest, you need a recipe that gives these delicious birds a chance to grow more tender. This is a tart and tangy recipe, but if you prefer sweeter sauces, add 1 or 2 tablespoons of brown sugar to the chicken bouillon.

CROSS QUAIL AND MILK GRAVY

6 quail
2 cups milk
4 beef bouillon cubes
2 cups water
2 cups peanut oil
2 cups self-rising flour
1 teaspoon seasoned salt
2 tablespoons self-rising flour

Serves 6

Marinate the quail in the milk in a large bowl for 30 to 45 minutes. Dissolve the bouillon cubes in the water in a bowl. Heat oil to 350 degrees in a deep heavy skillet. Remove the quail from the milk, reserving the milk. Coat with 2 cups flour mixed with seasoned salt. Fry, covered, in hot oil until golden brown, turning occasionally. Drain most of the oil. Stir in 2 tablespoons flour. Cook until the flour is browned, stirring constantly. Add the bouillon and reserved milk to the skillet. Cook until thickened, stirring constantly.

CRISPY QUAIL

12 quail, split in half along the
breastbone, back removed
Salt and pepper to taste
3 cups buttermilk
2 tablespoons Tabasco sauce
1/4 cup Dijon mustard
2 cups flour
1 cup Japanese breadcrumbs
(or substitute any breadcrumbs)
2 tablespoons salt
2 tablespoons garlic powder
1 tablespoon pepper
Oil for frying

Serves 4

Season split quail halves with salt and pepper. In a large bowl, combine buttermilk, Tabasco and mustard and blend until smooth. In another bowl, combine remaining ingredients except oil and stir. Place quail in buttermilk mixture, then flour mixture, then back to buttermilk, then into the flour mixture again. You're double-dipping your quail.

Heat oil to 360 to 370 degrees in a large, heavy pot. Using tongs, carefully place (not splash!) quail halves, 2 or 3 at a time, into the hot oil. Fry until golden brown, about 3 to 4 minutes. Remove and drain on paper towels.

Note: I've had folks tell me about how they soak their quail in buttermilk or saltwater to take out the gamey flavor. If your quail is gamey, it's probably been mishandled and may not be fit to eat, buttermilk or not. When in doubt, throw it out.

SFL

I grew up in Virginia when we still had coveys of wild bobwhite quail and knew where to find them. I went to college in Tucson, Arizona, in the mid-seventies and found huge numbers of Gambel's quail. Although huntable populations of quail are harder to come by, they're still my favorite bird to hunt and eat. Please don't pack your quail around in a game bag on a hot October day. Stop by the cooler and get them on ice ASAP.

GRILLED QUAIL WITH ROASTED PEPPER RELISH

1 pound quail (breasts and legs segmented)
Extra-virgin olive oil
Kosher salt or sea salt to taste
Freshly ground pepper to taste

Roasted Pepper Relish
1 cup roasted red bell peppers, coarsely chopped
1/4 cup extra-virgin olive oil
2 garlic cloves, minced
1 tablespoon fresh flat-leaf parsley, minced
1 teaspoon fresh thyme, minced
1 teaspoon anchovy, minced (optional)
Salt and freshly ground pepper to taste

Serves 4

Rub the quail with olive oil. Season with kosher salt and freshly ground pepper.

Grill or pan sear quail until the breast is medium-rare and the legs are medium. Season with salt and pepper to taste. Serve with the roasted pepper relish.

The Relish: Mix the roasted peppers, olive oil, garlic, parsley, thyme and anchovy together in a bowl. Season with salt and pepper.

MARINATED QUAIL

4 quail, whole, cleaned (2 per person, at least)
1/2 cup extra-virgin olive oil
2 garlic cloves, crushed
3 tablespoons balsamic vinegar
4 sprigs of fresh thyme (or 1 tablespoon dried)
2 sprigs fresh rosemary (or 1 teaspoon dried)
4 sprigs of fresh parsley
Salt and freshly ground pepper to taste

Serves 2

Mix all ingredients together in a container. Cover and refrigerate at least 4 hours. When ready to prepare, remove quail from marinade, discarding the marinade. Grill the quail until medium-rare or medium. Serve while hot.

This is one of those simple tasty dishes you can mostly prepare ahead of time, pack away in a container set in an ice chest, and pull out to grill when you're ready for dinner. Perfect for a day at the lake or camping overnight. Serve with a seasonal grilled vegetable and some foil-roasted potatoes, and you have another campsite gourmet treat.

MARINATED QUAIL WITH PECAN PESTO VINAIGRETTE

Quail

1/2 cup olive oil

1 cup chicken broth

2 lemons, juice only

1/2 cup onion, sliced

4 garlic cloves, minced

1 teaspoon Dijon mustard

1 tablespoon Italian seasoning

4 to 6 quail, or 2 pheasant, quartered

Pecan Pesto Vinaigrette

1/2 cup pecan pieces, roasted in a
325-degree oven until
slightly browned

2 garlic cloves, chopped

1 cup fresh basil leaves

1 lemon, juice only

1/4 cup Parmesan cheese

1/2 cup olive oil

1/3 cup white wine vinegar

Salt and pepper

Serves 4

The Marinade: Combine all ingredients in a bowl. Place quail pieces in a ceramic, plastic or glass dish and add the marinade. Cover and refrigerate, turning occasionally. Marinate for 6 to 12 hours. To cook, remove leg/thigh sections and place in a well-oiled baking dish. Pour marinade over. Cover with foil and bake in a 375-degree oven for 1 hour. Add breast pieces, cover and bake for 20 minutes more or until quail breast pieces are just cooked.

The Vinaigrette: Process pecan pieces, garlic, basil, lemon and a few tablespoons of the olive oil in a food processor or blender until a paste is formed. Add Parmesan cheese and vinegar. Pulse to blend. While motor is running, add remaining oil in a thin stream until emulsified. Season with salt and pepper.

The Assembly: Arrange quail pieces on plates and drizzle with the vinaigrette.

SFL

If your bird has been frozen for awhile, it just might need a little help. Freezing tends to dry out meats, especially if you have not caught on to the vacuum-packaging thing. If you don't have a vacuum-packaging machine, go get one now. One of the best ways to help out a tired old frozen bird is with a good marinade. Marinades will add flavor to meats that are long past fresh. Don't use marinades to cover up foods that either look bad or smell bad. There's a reason they got that way and they should be disposed of. I like to serve this with rice.

WHITE-ON-WHITE CHILI

1 cup white navy beans
7 cups water
4 teaspoons chicken
bouillon granules
1/2 yellow onion, chopped
1 garlic clove, minced
2 tablespoons oil
1 garlic clove, minced
1/2 yellow onion, chopped
1 teaspoon dried leaf oregano
1/2 teaspoon ground cumin
1/2 teaspoon salt
1/4 teaspoon chili powder
1/4 teaspoon cayenne pepper
2 pounds quail meat, diced
(5 to 6 cups)
2 whole canned chile peppers, diced
1/4 cup cream
1/2 cup (2 ounces) grated Monterey
Jack cheese

Serves 6

Start at least the day before, or as many as 5 or 6 days ahead. Soak the beans in 3 cups of the water overnight. Drain the beans, rinse well, and transfer to a large pot. Add 4 cups water water, the bouillon granules, 1/2 onion, and 1 garlic clove to the beans. Bring to a boil, reduce the heat to a simmer and cover the pot. Let the beans cook for 2 hours, until they are tender. Set aside until you are ready to assemble the chili.

In a 3-quart Dutch oven, heat the oil over medium heat and sauté 1 garlic clove and 1/2 onion until tender. Stir in oregano, cumin, salt, chili powder and cayenne pepper.

When you begin to smell the spices, add the diced quail meat and sauté until the meat is opaque. Add the chile peppers and cooked beans (with cooking liquid) and bring the saucepan back up to a simmer. Add the cream and cook until the chili is hot again. Serve hot in soup bowls with a generous sprinkle of cheese on top.

EMC

One of the great things about going to the Helena, Montana, gun show is the endless crock of white chili O'Brien's has simmering away at the snack bar. This pot isn't endless, but it's a delicious variation on that classic favorite.

GRILLED QUAIL BREASTS, CHEESE AND PROSCIUTTO

8 boneless quail breasts, split, skin on or off
2 tablespoons olive oil
1 tablespoon Italian seasoning
Salt and pepper to taste
8 thin slices prosciutto
8 (½-inch) cubes hard cheese (like Swiss, Gruyère, dry Jack, etc.)

Serves 4 as appetizers

Combine quail breasts, olive oil, Italian seasoning and salt and pepper in a small bowl. Toss to coat, cover and refrigerate for 1 to 2 hours.

Soak 8 small wooden skewers in water for 30 minutes. Lay prosciutto flat on a clean work surface or cutting board. For each slice, place a quail breast half on one end of the prosciutto. Place a piece of cheese on the quail breast and top the cheese with another quail breast half.

Roll up the prosciutto snugly and secure with a skewer, making sure that you spear through both ends of the prosciutto and the cheese. Place on a medium-hot grill until lightly browned on all sides and quail breasts are just cooked and still slightly pink.

SFL

If you can't find prosciutto (a dry-seasoned, cured Italian ham), use partially cooked bacon. The recipe calls for quail breasts only. This doesn't mean that you throw away the rest of the bird. Season the legs the same as the breasts and toss them on the grill as well. The bodies are great for making soups and broth.

The total weight of a clutch of eggs produced by some duck species can equal or exceed the female's weight.

The Challenge
Jim Hansel

Jim's love of wildlife and the outdoors has been the subject of his artwork for many years. However, Jim's ability to paint these images has not come without its challenges. The world we see is not always the world Jim sees.

In 1972, at the age of twelve, Jim was diagnosed with a degenerative eye condition which left him legally blind. Despite his visual limitations, he has learned to create beautifully detailed images with the use of magnifiers and low-vision aids. As Jim paints in the detail work on a painting, he is working only one or two inches away from the canvas.

Since the release of his first image in 1987, Jim has produced nearly 100 limited-edition prints, many of which are sold out. His reputation for detail and his distinctive, colorful landscapes have proven to be very popular with art collectors across the country.

ROASTED QUAIL STUFFED WITH CORN BREAD STUFFING

1/4 cup (1/2 stick) butter
3/4 cup yellow onion, finely diced
1 cup celery, finely diced
1/4 cup fresh parsley, finely chopped
1 tablespoon chopped fresh sage, or
1 1/2 teaspoons dried
2 teaspoons fresh thyme,
finely chopped, or 1 teaspoon dried
3 cups small pieces or diced
corn bread, toasted
1 1/2 cups chicken stock
8 whole cleaned quail
2 tablespoons extra-virgin olive oil
Salt and freshly ground
pepper to taste

Serves 4 (2 per person)

Melt butter in a medium sauté pan over medium-high heat. Add onion and celery and sauté until tender. Toss in herbs and continue cooking for about another minute. Remove from heat.

Place corn bread in a large bowl. Add the onion mixture and chicken stock and mix well. When mix is well combined and cool, begin stuffing the quail cavity with about 1/2 cup or more of stuffing to each bird. Tie the legs together with butcher's string to hold stuffing in while cooking.

Rub birds with olive oil and season with salt and pepper. Roast at 375 degrees for about 15 to 20 minutes. Cut string before serving. Serve with any extra stuffing.

LMF

CROSS SMOKED TURKEY

1 wild turkey
1/2 cup peanut oil
1 teaspoon white pepper
1 cup sparkling lemon-lime soda
1 cup honey

Serves 8 to 12

Brush the turkey with peanut oil and sprinkle with white pepper. Place a piece of wide heavy-duty aluminum foil in a large roasting pan. Place turkey breast side up on foil. Pour the lemon-lime soda into cavity of turkey. Seal foil tightly. Bake at 300 degrees for 8 minutes per pound. Remove from the oven.

Melt the honey over low heat in a saucepan. Baste the turkey with honey. Place on greased aluminum foil on the grill. Smoke at medium over hickory chips until turkey is golden brown.

BJC

HOWELL FRIED TURKEY STRIPS

6 wild turkey breast strips,
cut 3/4 inch thick and
1 inch wide
Several cloves of garlic, peeled, cut
in half and slightly crushed
3 tablespoons each ground black
pepper and salt, mixed together
Milk
Chef's Grill Plus® instant marinade
3 teaspoons butter
3 tablespoons olive oil
Flour

Serves 2

Score the breast strips all over with a sharp knife or perforate with a fork. Rub each strip on both sides with a cut garlic clove. Shake the ground black pepper and salt mixture onto both sides of the strips.

Prepare a milk wash by mixing 3 parts milk to 1 part Chef's Grill Plus (www.chefsgrillplus.com). Dip the strips in the milk wash. Place in a sealable plastic bag with flour and shake until fully coated.

Melt the butter and olive oil in a large cast-iron skillet. When the mixture of oil and butter is hot, add the turkey strips. Fry them on each side, about 3 minutes in all.

Serve hot and enjoy.

 Henderson Park Inn

The Beach Walk restaurant at the Henderson Park Inn, Destin, Florida, features game and freshly caught fish on its daily menu. The Inn is known for exceptional service . . . to be challenged only by the exceptional tastes.

WILD TURKEY WITH CAPERS AND MUSHROOMS

1 large boneless skinless turkey breast, halved and sliced on the bias in about 1/4- to 1/2-inch slices
1 cup flour
3 tablespoons (about) extra-virgin olive oil
Salt and pepper to taste
1 1/2 cups domestic or wild mushrooms, sliced
2 tablespoons shallots, minced
2 tablespoons capers (optional)
2 tablespoons fresh Italian flat-leaf parsley, finely chopped
Juice of 1/2 lemon (Meyer lemon is suggested if available)
1/2 cup chardonnay or other white wine
3/4 cup chicken stock
3 tablespoons butter

Serves 2 to 4

Dredge the turkey slices in flour. Shake off excess. In a medium sauté pan, heat olive oil over medium-high heat. Season turkey slices with salt and pepper. Add to oil in pan. Sauté until golden brown on both sides. Remove from pan. (You do not need to fry the turkey to death, that will just dry out the turkey slices.) Set turkey aside and keep warm.

Return pan to heat. Add a little more olive oil if needed. Add mushrooms, sauté for about 2 minutes. Add shallots and sauté for about 1 minute. Lower heat and pull pan away from fire if shallots brown quickly; be careful not to burn them. Next, throw in the capers, parsley and lemon juice.

Deglaze the pan (pick up all the nice tasty golden pieces on the bottom of the pan) by adding the white wine. Add the stock and reduce the liquid by half. Remove from heat and swirl in butter 1 tablespoon at a time. Wait for each tablespoon to melt into the sauce before adding another. Swirling it in away from the heat will keep your sauce from becoming greasy. Pour sauce over golden turkey slices and serve.

Note: This goes great with rice. If you're cooking it up in the spring time, some fresh grilled asparagus would be a perfect complement.

LMF

This recipe is always a favorite. If you are not a fan of capers, just omit them from the recipe. Either way you end up with a dish that will please even the fussiest of eaters. Prepare this for a friend or family member that is convinced wild turkey is unpleasant to eat. They will be amazed by your culinary talent. Just don't overcook the turkey!

WILD TURKEY TAMALES

2 cups masa harina flour
2/3 cup melted shortening
1 1/4 cups warm chicken broth
1/2 teaspoon salt
2 tablespoons vegetable oil
1/3 cup onion, diced
1 cup fresh tomatillos or green
tomatoes, quartered (optional)
2 garlic cloves, minced
1 jalapeño chile, seeded and minced
1 teaspoon chile powder
1/2 teaspoon ground cumin
1/4 teaspoon salt
2 cups cooked wild turkey breast, cut
into 1/2-inch cubes or shredded
16 corn husks, soaked in water for
at least 1 hour
Large pot with lid and steamer
basket or perforated insert

Makes about 16 small tamales

Combine the flour, shortening, broth and 1/2 teaspoon salt in a bowl and mix using a fork or your hands until the consistency of moist cookie dough. If it's too dry, add a little more broth. If it's too wet, mix in a little more flour.

In a large skillet, heat oil over medium heat. Add onion, tomatillos, garlic and jalapeño and sauté for 3 to 4 minutes. Add chile powder, cumin, 1/4 teaspoon salt and turkey breast and stir to blend flavors. Simmer for 2 to 3 minutes and then allow to cool.

For each tamale, lay a corn husk on a flat surface with the narrow end pointing toward you. Take about 2 to 3 tablespoons of the flour mixture and spread evenly along the bottom quarter of the corn husk, about 1/2 inch from any edge of the husk. In the center of the flour mixture, place a few tablespoons of the turkey mixture. Fold the left edge of the husk over the stuffing. The idea is to surround the stuffing with flour mixture. Fold the right edge over and fold the bottom up toward the center.

Place in a hot steamer basket in a large pot with a water level just under the bottom of the basket. Place tamales folded-side-down in the basket, leaving a little room between each so that steam can cook each one. Add water as they steam, if necessary. Tamales will take from 25 to 40 minutes to steam, depending on how big they are. They will be soft, moist and hot when cooked and will firm up as they start to cool.

SFL

reat with any wild game. You could also slow roast deer neck and shoulder roast, shred the meat, and wrap it up in the tamales.

WOODCOCK WANT-NOTS

Breasts of several woodcock
1 water chestnut for each breast half
1/3 slice bacon for each wrap

Serves 1 per bird

Soak wooden skewers in cold water for 30 minutes. Bone the breast meat from the woodcock, saving the tenderloin for another use. Lay each woodcock breast half on a cutting board and with the palm of your hand press it flat, and just a bit longer, so it will wrap around the chestnut. Then wrap that with 1/3 slice of bacon, and run a skewer through the thickest part.

Preheat the grill to medium. When the grill is ready, arrange the bacon-wrapped woodcock breasts on the grill and cook about 5 to 8 minutes, turning often, until still pink in the middle and the bacon is browned. Serve immediately, either alone or with chips and dip.

EMC

Here's a recipe that fits right into the hurly-burly of hunting camp. Doesn't matter if you have one bird or four, as long as you have a can of water chestnuts around and a little bacon, you can make a quick appetizer to tide you over until dinner's ready. Notice that even non-cooks can do this one. But please don't overcook the woodcock—they're delicious when slightly pink. Well done and they'll develop a "livery" flavor.

CHUKAR ITALIANO

1 cup chopped onion
2 teaspoons diced garlic
2 tablespoons oil
1 (14-ounce) can whole
peeled tomatoes
1 tablespoon chopped fresh basil
(or 1 teaspoon dried leaf)
2 teaspoons capers, drained
1 tablespoon chopped black olives
Deboned breasts of 2 chukars, sliced
across the grain
1/2 teaspoon salt
1/4 teaspoon pepper
Hot cooked pasta (optional)

Serves 4

In a large skillet, sauté the onion and garlic in oil over medium heat until they begin to brown, about 5 minutes. Add the tomatoes, breaking them up in the skillet.

Once the tomatoes start to simmer, add the basil, capers, olives, sliced chukar, salt and pepper. Reduce the heat to low, cover the skillet, and simmer about 10 minutes. Serve over pasta, or with garlic bread.

EMC

A robust, flavorful dish with the meat of one of the West's best-kept secrets. If you don't have chukars, you can substitute any tender, white-meated bird. Quail will work, as will grouse; just be sure to have about 6 to 8 ounces (1 to 1½ cups) of boneless meat to fill out this dish.

Venison & Other Big Game

Deer · Elk · Boar · Bison

Fare Game

BASIC BIG GAME STEW

2 cans or bottles flat beer
1/4 cup Worcestershire sauce
1/3 teaspoon freshly ground
black pepper
6 garlic cloves, minced
4 cups game meat, skinned,
deboned and cut into 1-inch cubes
2 tablespoons vegetable oil
1 yellow onion, coarsely chopped
2 carrots, diced
2 ribs celery, diced
2 unpeeled red potatoes, diced into
1-inch cubes
1 (14-ounce) can diced tomatoes
(with juice)
8 cups (2 quarts) beef broth

Serves 6 to 8

Combine beer with next 3 ingredients in a glass or plastic bowl. Add meat, toss gently. Cover and refrigerate for 6 to 12 hours. Remove meat from marinade, reserve marinade.

Heat oil in a heavy-duty stockpot over medium-high heat. Add meat and cook until browned evenly. Add onion, carrots and celery. Cook for 3 to 5 minutes. Add potatoes, reserved marinade, diced tomatoes and broth. Bring to a boil. Reduce heat to low, cover and simmer until meat falls apart when poked with a spoon, about 2 to 3 hours.

SFL

Fare Game

CROSS VENISON SOUP

3 pounds venison, cut into small
stewing pieces
12 cups (3 quarts) cold water
2 carrots
1 rib celery
1 tablespoon salt
1 tablespoon pepper
1 tablespoon chopped parsley
4 green onions
2 large potatoes, diced
Dash of Tabasco sauce

Serves 8 to 10

Combine the venison and cold water in a stockpot. Bring to a boil over medium-high heat. Add the carrots, celery, salt, pepper, parsley, green onions and potatoes. Simmer, covered, until meat is tender. Season with the Tabasco sauce.

BJC

SLOW-SIMMERED VENISON CHILI

2 pounds ground venison
3 tablespoons vegetable oil
2 (16-ounce) cans kidney beans
2 (8-ounce) cans tomato sauce
3 tablespoons chili powder
1/2 teaspoon cayenne pepper, or
to taste
1/2 teaspoon garlic powder
1/2 teaspoon oregano
1/2 teaspoon salt
2 teaspoons ground cumin
1/2 cup minced dried onions
1 cup (or more) water

Serves 6

Brown the venison in hot oil in a medium pot. Add the kidney beans, tomato sauce, chili powder, cayenne, garlic powder, oregano, salt, cumin, onions and water and mix well. Simmer for 1 1/2 hours, stirring occasionally. Add additional water if chili is too thick.

BJC

CHIPOTLE VENISON BURGER

1¹/₂ pounds ground venison
¹/₄ cup yellow onion, minced
3 garlic cloves, minced
2 tablespoons brown sugar
1 teaspoon kosher salt
1 teaspoon black pepper
1 tablespoon dried Italian seasoning
2 tablespoons chipotle chiles with
adobo sauce, minced
4 slices Pepper Jack cheese
4 sturdy burger buns or
Kaiser rolls, split
4 large lettuce leaves
4 slices tomato

Serves 4

Combine ground venison with next 7 ingredients and mix well. Form into 4 patties about ³/₄ inch thick. Place on a white-hot, well-oiled barbecue grill and brown evenly on both sides, about 4 minutes per side. Melt cheese over top before removing from grill. Place in buns with lettuce, tomato and your choice of condiments.

Note: You can make burgers out of any type of waterfowl as well. Just place chopped meat in a food processor and pulse until it is about the size of a garbanzo bean. Blend with ground pork or beef.

SғL

*B*ust out the 'cue and ice down the beer—it's officially grilling season. Oh sure, in most of the Western U.S., you can fire up the barbecue just about any time during the year, but now's the time when I end up cooking outside more often than in. Keep the kitchen cool and fire up some of these delicious fiery deer burgers. If your processor hasn't added some fat to your venison burger, mix in 20 to 30 percent additional fatty ground beef or pork.

Fare Game

Venison, Mushroom and Blue Cheese Burger

2 tablespoons butter
1 onion, finely diced
2 garlic cloves, minced
2 cups mushrooms, coarsely chopped
1½ pounds ground venison
½ cup blue cheese crumbles
2 tablespoons bread crumbs
Salt and pepper to taste
4 burger buns, split
4 lettuce leaves
4 slices tomato

Makes 4 big burgers

Melt butter in a medium skillet over medium heat. Add onion and garlic and sauté until onion is translucent. Stir in mushrooms and sauté until soft. Transfer to a medium bowl and allow to cool. Add ground venison, blue cheese, bread crumbs, salt and pepper and mix well with your hands to blend. Form into 4 large patties. Grill, pan-fry or broil patties until browned. Add to bun with lettuce and tomato.

S_FL

I often add some ground fatty meat to my ground venison to add flavor and moisture. Here I used a creamy cheese, onion, and mushrooms for flavor. You'll discover freshly ground meat tastes better than frozen. You can also grind thawed frozen meat before cooking.

Sweet Heat Venison Meatballs

3 tablespoons extra-virgin olive oil
1 small yellow onion, minced
2 garlic cloves, minced
2 tablespoons Italian seasoning
½ cup fresh flat-leaf Italian parsley, finely chopped
2 pounds ground venison
3 eggs
½ cup heavy cream or half-and-half
1 cup fine bread crumbs
¼ cup (1 ounce) freshly grated Parmesan cheese
Salt and freshly ground pepper to taste
1½ cups barbecue sauce
1 tablespoon lemon juice
1 teaspoon Tabasco sauce

Serves 4 to 6

Heat olive oil in a medium sauté pan over medium-high heat. Add onion and sauté until caramelized and golden brown. Add garlic, Italian seasoning and parsley and sauté for 1 minute. Remove from heat and set aside until cool.

In a medium bowl, incorporate the next 5 ingredients with the cooled onion mixture. Season with salt and pepper and mix well. Roll into bite-size meatballs. Bake in a shallow roasting pan at 375 degrees for 25 minutes or until medium. Check them after 15 to 20 minutes to make sure they don't dry out or overcook. Combine the last 3 ingredients and cook over medium heat until warm. Serve the meatballs hot with warm barbecue sauce for dipping.

L_MF

VENISON SUGO (GRAVY) ON CHEESE RAVIOLI

5 tablespoons extra-virgin olive oil
1 pound ground venison, or a nicely
trimmed and deboned roast,
cut into chunks
Kosher salt and freshly
ground pepper to taste
1 yellow onion, finely diced
3 garlic cloves, minced
1 cup mushrooms, sliced (optional)
1 teaspoon freshly chopped
rosemary, or 1/2 teaspoon dried
1/2 cup fresh flat-leaf Italian parsley,
finely chopped
2 teaspoons fresh thyme, minced,
or 1 teaspoon dried
1 cup red wine
16 ounces canned stewed tomatoes
2 cups water
1 tablespoon tomato paste
Pinch of crushed red pepper
(optional)
2 tablespoons fresh basil, chopped
2 pounds fresh or frozen cheese
ravioli, cooked
3 cups (12 ounces) freshly grated
Parmesan cheese

Serves 4

Heat 3 tablespoons of the olive oil over medium-high heat in a large stockpot. Season venison with salt and pepper. Sauté in the oil until brown. Remove meat and set aside.

Return pot to heat, add remaining 2 tablespoons olive oil. Add onion and sauté until golden brown. Add garlic and sauté for 1 minute. Add mushrooms, rosemary, parsley and thyme and sauté for 2 more minutes.

Return meat to pot. Stir. Add a splash of the wine to deglaze the pan and stir with a wooden spoon. Add the undrained tomatoes, water, tomato paste and the remaining red wine. Stir and reduce heat to a low simmer. Stir occasionally and let simmer for about 2 1/2 hours. Add the crushed red pepper flakes and adjust seasonings if needed. Remove from heat and stir in basil; keep warm. Spoon venison gravy over ravioli and sprinkle with freshly grated cheese.

LMF

Growing up, this was always my favorite side dish my Uncle Jerry would prepare to accompany our traditional Thanksgiving dinner. By the time you finished a healthy helping of these raviolis and big slices of my Aunt Linda's hot oven-baked bread, you didn't think you had much room left for the other fixings. Somehow we managed! Try it as an addition to your next winter holiday meal.

Venison Breakfast Steaks

Garlic Sauce
3 tablespoons extra-virgin olive oil
1 tablespoon fresh garlic, minced
Salt to taste
1/2 cup (1 stick) unsalted butter,
at room temperature

Venison
2 cups bread crumbs
1/4 cup fresh parsley, minced
1 teaspoon fresh thyme, minced
4 (4-ounce) venison medallions,
trimmed and pounded flat
1 teaspoon kosher salt
Freshly ground pepper to taste
1/2 cup all-purpose flour
1 cup buttermilk
1 cup extra-virgin olive oil

Serves 4

The Sauce: Heat olive oil in a small saucepan. Add garlic and sauté for about 1 minute, just long enough to infuse the flavor of the garlic into the oil without burning. Add salt and butter and heat until the butter melts. Keep warm until ready to serve.

The Venison: In a bowl, combine bread crumbs, parsley and thyme. Season venison with salt and pepper. Dredge venison in flour. Dip into buttermilk, then into bread crumb mixture. Shake off excess. Place into hot olive oil in frying pan. Cook quickly over medium-high heat until golden brown. Do not overcook, try to keep meat to just under medium. Remove from pan and drain on paper towels. Serve with garlic butter sauce drizzled over steaks.

LMF

This recipe was one of my favorite breakfast dishes my grandmother would make me in the fall. Don't be afraid of the garlic sauce in the morning, just make sure everyone else has some, too. Try this with all the homemade fixings of potatoes and if you really want to put in the extra effort, prepare homemade biscuits with white gravy from the pan drippings. Oh my!

Ducks Unlimited® has conserved more than 4,130,000 acres
of wetlands in the United States, more than 6,680,000 in Canada,
and more than 1,800,000 in Mexico.

PAN-SEARED VENISON MEDALLIONS WITH BALSAMIC BERRY SAUCE

2 pounds well-trimmed venison
medallions, about 4 inches wide by
1/2 inch thick (see sidebar)
Salt and pepper to taste
2 tablespoons olive oil
1/2 teaspoon fresh rosemary
leaves, minced
2 garlic cloves, minced
1/4 cup dry red wine
1/2 cup balsamic vinegar
1 tablespoon plum preserves
3 tablespoons cold butter,
cut into pieces
3/4 cup fresh berries, any kind
1/4 cup blue cheese crumbles

Serves 4

Season meat evenly with salt and pepper. Heat olive oil in a large skillet over medium-high heat. Add meat and brown on each side, about 1 or 2 minutes per side, but not past rare. Add rosemary, garlic, wine, balsamic vinegar and plum preserves. Remove meat after 1 minute and keep warm. Reduce liquid to a few tablespoons. Whisk in cold butter until melted. Immediately remove pan from heat and stir in berries. Arrange medallions on plates, spoon sauce over and top with blue cheese crumbles.

SFL

Although the recipe calls for "pan-seared" venison medallions, the medallions can also be grilled or broiled as long as you don't overcook them. When using hindquarter cuts, slice the meat with the grain into strips about 4 inches wide. Slice across the grain of each piece, about 1/2 inch wide, to make the medallions.

PEPPERCORN-ENCRUSTED FALLOW DEER WITH DIJON SAGE CREAM SAUCE

4 (10-ounce) fallow deer tenderloin or back strap medallions, trimmed
Sea salt or kosher salt to taste
Dijon mustard for coating
1/2 cup cracked or crushed black peppercorns
3 tablespoons (about) good-quality extra-virgin olive oil
2 tablespoons fresh shallots, minced
1 teaspoon fresh sage, minced
1/2 cup chardonnay
2 tablespoons Dijon mustard
1/2 cup chicken stock (salt-free)
3/4 cup heavy cream
2 teaspoons fresh Italian flat-leaf parsley, minced

Serves 4

Season the meat with salt. Apply a thin layer of Dijon mustard to coat one side of each medallion. Place peppercorns onto a plate. Press the peppercorns onto the mustard side of the meat until they stick. Set aside.

Heat 3 tablespoons olive oil in a large sauté pan over medium-high heat. When oil is hot, but not smoking, place medallions in pan. You should hear a nice sizzle. Sear each side and cook until rare or medium-rare. Remove the medallion from the pan, lightly tent with foil and set aside. Reserve the pan drippings. Return the pan to heat and add the shallots. Sauté for about 1 minute. Add a touch of additional oil if necessary to pan. Add the sage and sauté quickly. Add the chardonnay. When the wine is reduced by half, add 2 tablespoons Dijon mustard and chicken stock. Reduce and then add the cream. Reduce to the desired thickness. Add the parsley, sauté quickly and remove from heat. Serve over the fallow deer medallions.

Note: A natural wine pairing for this recipe would be an earthy cabernet with hints of peppercorn. However, since a buttery chardonnay is used as an ingredient in this recipe, it creates a bridge for the same chardonnay to be a perfect pairing to the dish as well. It is a matter of personal preference and finding the balance that will enhance the complementing flavors.

LMF

I developed this recipe for wildlife artist John Banovich's art reception at the Dallas Safari Club Convention in January 2009. It was a huge hit with his guests, and it is still going strong for new audiences. It is my twist and a loose variation of the classic French recipe, steak au poivre. The fact that I use fallow deer makes it outstanding.

VENISON WITH CRANBERRY SWEET-AND-SOUR SAUCE

1 bottle dry red wine
1/2 cup balsamic vinegar
1 pound fresh cranberries
Juice of 1 lemon
2 sprigs of rosemary
1 shallot, minced
1/4 cup brown sugar
1 tablespoon cornstarch mixed with
equal part cold water
Salt and white pepper to taste
4 (6- to 8-ounce) venison steaks,
trimmed of all fat, gristle and bone

Serves 4

In a large saucepan, combine red wine and next 5 ingredients. Bring to a boil over medium-high heat, uncovered. Lower to medium heat and reduce liquid by half. Remove rosemary and allow mixture to cool. When cooled, transfer contents to a blender or food processor and purée. (Do not attempt to process the hot sauce in the blender or processor! It has to be cool. As soon as you turn on the machine, hot liquid cranberry sauce will spew out of the top and burn you and/or make a really big mess.)

Return processed sauce to the saucepan and add brown sugar and half the cornstarch mixture. Heat to boiling. Add additional cornstarch mixture to thicken, if needed. Adjust sweet and sour flavors as desired by adding additional balsamic vinegar (sour) or brown sugar (sweet). Season with salt and pepper.

Season venison with salt and pepper. Grill, broil or pan-sear until medium-rare. Spoon a little sauce on each plate. Slice venison across the grain and arrange slices over sauce. Garnish with additional cranberries, fresh herbs, orange slices, etc.

SFL

Cooking with cranberries during the holiday season makes me feel all warm and fuzzy inside. Cranberries are a decent source of vitamin C and potassium. They are supposedly good for blood circulation, the digestive system, the urinary tract, and the complexion, although I wouldn't recommend rubbing them over your face. I like them because they taste and look good. Pop a fresh cranberry in your mouth. Go ahead—try it! Not too good is it? They are a bit tart, so it's best to pair them with something sweet, in this case brown sugar, to balance the acidic tartness. You may want to save a few of the cooked cranberries for garnish before processing the rest in the blender.

GRILLED VENISON WITH BEERBECUE SAUCE

2 to 2½ pounds venison steaks,
loins, etc. (see sidebar)
1 tablespoon seasoned pepper
1 tablespoon seasoned salt
3 cloves fresh garlic, minced
Beerbecue Sauce (below)

Serves 6

Season meat with next 3 ingredients. Cover and refrigerate for 1 hour. Grill over hot coals to rare or medium-rare. Just before meat is removed from the grill, baste with a little beerbecue sauce. Serve beerbecue sauce on the side or drizzled over a portion of the meat. Allow meat to rest a few minutes before slicing.

BEERBECUE SAUCE

2 tablespoons butter
1 yellow onion, finely diced
2 tablespoons brown sugar
2 garlic cloves, minced
1 (12-ounce) can flat beer
(I prefer dark beer)
1 lemon, sliced into rings
3 tablespoons Worcestershire sauce
1 cup tomato purée
½ teaspoon liquid smoke
¼ cup cider vinegar
Salt and freshly ground pepper
to taste

Makes approximately 2 cups

Melt butter in a saucepan over medium heat. Add onion and cook until translucent. Add brown sugar and garlic and cook for 2 to 3 minutes. Add remaining ingredients except salt and pepper. Stir well, bring to a boil and then simmer until sauce thickens. The sauce should be the consistency of thick tomato sauce. Taste and season with salt and pepper as desired.

SFL

I've also used this barbecue sauce on grilled fish, upland game, and just about anything else that works on the 'cue. I often grill any cut of deer from the loin to the hams. The "secret" is to remove anything that's not muscle. After grilling to no more than medium-rare, slice the meat across the grain to serve.

TEXAS-STYLE POT-ROASTED VENISON

1 (4-pound) venison roast
3 tablespoons peanut oil
6 garlic cloves, sliced
1 envelope onion soup mix
12 ounces cola

Serves 6 to 8

Score the roast in several places. Rub the peanut oil over roast. Poke holes in roast with a small knife and insert the garlic. Spread the soup mix over the roast. Place a large sheet of aluminum foil in a roasting pan. Place the roast on the foil. Pour cola around the roast. Seal foil tightly. Bake at 300 degrees for 3 hours.

BJC

DEER FLANK WITH ASPARAGUS

4 deer flank steaks,
membrane removed
Kosher salt and freshly ground
black pepper to taste
4 thin slices prosciutto
16 asparagus spears, blanched
and cooled
1 cup (4 ounces) grated
Parmesan cheese
Olive oil

Serves 4

Place steak on a flat surface with the narrow end toward you. Season both sides with salt and pepper. Place 1 slice of prosciutto over the steak. Place 4 asparagus spears together on the narrow end of the steak. Sprinkle cheese over asparagus and prosciutto. Grasp the lower end of the steak and roll firmly over the asparagus. Continue rolling to the end and secure with toothpicks. Spread olive oil over outside and season with additional salt and pepper. Cook on a grill or in a hot, oiled pan for 2 or 3 minutes per side or until cheese starts to melt and meat is rare to medium-rare. To serve, slice in half. Remove toothpicks.

SFL

Venison flank steaks are cut from the abdominal section. They're thin and tender, but often discarded by processors. Before cooking, remove the thin membrane that surrounds the flank. On flank steaks from larger animals, it helps to gently pound them until the meat is about 1/4 inch thick throughout.

OLD WORLD MARINATED VENISON AND POTATO KABOBS

1 pound venison, cut into
2-inch chunks
1/4 cup malt vinegar
2 tablespoons brown sugar
2 tablespoons Dijon mustard
2 tablespoons oil
1/2 teaspoon coarse black pepper
1 pound new red potatoes
1 red onion, sliced thick
4 slices bacon

Serves 2 to 4

Trim the steak chunks, and dry with paper towels. In a sealable plastic bag, combine the vinegar, sugar, mustard, oil and pepper. Add the meat and refrigerate 24 to 48 hours.

Preheat the grill to medium-high heat. Microwave the potatoes on High for about 2 minutes or just until fork-tender, but still firm enough to be able to put on skewers. Remove the meat from the marinade and arrange on the skewers, alternating with the potatoes and onion slices and threading the bacon along the skewer as you add ingredients.

Cook about 2 minutes per side, until the bacon is browned all over, turning four times. Remove from the skewers and serve hot with more mustard.

Note: New potatoes are the golf-ball–size, first-picked potatoes that show up in the produce section in early summer. You can cut up mature potatoes for these kabobs, but new potatoes have better flavor and don't need any prep.

EMC

For those who don't cotton to super-sweet barbecue sauces, this mustard sauce makes a vibrant statement. And the real joy of this recipe is it's a grilled version of a one-dish meal. No sides required.

Crossing the River
Bruce Miller

International Artist of the Year
—1999

Born in Minneapolis in 1952, Bruce Miller has experimented with a variety of genres including portraits, landscape, abstract, and surrealism. Being an avid outdoorsman and Eagle Scout, in 1981 he began painting wildlife. In 1988 he won his first national contest, Artist of the Year for the Michigan Wildlife Art Festival, and since has won more than fifty awards and been featured at several major art shows in the country. He has won twenty-three conservation stamps including the 1993 Federal Duck Stamp and the 2007 Texas Duck Stamp. He was named the 1999 Ducks Unlimited® International Artist of the Year for *Hooded Mergansers* and the Rocky Mountain Elk Foundation Artist of the Year in 2002. Miller's work has generated over $10,000,000 for conservation.

BRUCE MILLER
2001

CHEATIN' RIBS

2 to 3 pounds moose or elk ribs,
in sections
1 to 2 pounds pork ribs
2 tablespoons oil
2 (12-ounce) cans beer
12 ounces of your favorite
tomato-based barbecue sauce

Serves 6 to 8

Preheat the oven to 300 degrees. Separate the moose/elk ribs and dry with paper towels. Arrange them in the roasting pan so they make an even layer.

In a large skillet, brown the pork ribs in the oil over medium heat until just golden. Transfer them to the roasting pan, covering the game ribs.

In a large bowl, combine the beer and barbecue sauce. Pour over the ribs. (If you need more liquid to cover, mix more.) Cover the roasting pan and roast the ribs 2 to 3 hours or until tender.

Note: Because prepared barbecue sauces vary in salt and pepper content, it's best to not add any salt or pepper to the cooking sauce. Taste the ribs when they're done, and then you can add salt and pepper to taste at the table.

As for the beer, the most common ones, like Miller Genuine Draft, work very well. The trick to cooking ribs is first to have enough meat on the ribs to make cooking worthwhile. A trophy deer—whitetail or mule deer—or any moose or elk will provide lots of meat. However, you can pad the ribs by using the brisket and any other flank meat.

EMC

If you're new to ribs, or just like to keep things simple, this is the recipe for you. Choose a tomato-based barbecue sauce, but one with little if any smoke flavor. (The smoke will only intensify in the roasting and may get too strong.) Then just sit back and let the roaster do its stuff.

ELK WITH BARLEY SOUP

2 pounds elk meat or other game,
trimmed and cut into 1-inch cubes
Salt and pepper to taste
2 tablespoons vegetable oil
1 large onion, diced
4 stalks celery, diced
3 carrots, diced
4 garlic cloves, minced
8 cups (2 quarts) game broth or
beef broth
2 sprigs of fresh rosemary (optional)
3 cups cooked barley
(prepare as per package)

Serves 6 to 8

Season meat liberally with salt and pepper. Heat oil in a large stockpot over medium-high heat, add meat and brown evenly. Add onion, celery, carrots and garlic. Cook 5 minutes or until onion is translucent. Add broth and rosemary and cook over medium heat until meat is tender. Depending on the cut of meat, it may take an hour or two. Remove rosemary and stir in barley. Serve with warm bread or croutons.

SFL

I look forward to cold weather here in northern California so that I can enjoy a steaming bowl of soup. Any antlered game animal will do here. Also, try this recipe with ducks or geese, but save it for less-than-premium species like divers and snow geese. I cannot overemphasize how much better the soup will taste if you make your own broth or stock from the carcasses and trim of your animals. Roast 'em with some vegetables and throw everything into a pot. Cover it with water, bring to a boil, and simmer, uncovered, for 5 to 6 hours or, better yet, overnight. Save the liquid and discard the rest. This recipe calls for onion, carrots, and celery, but you can use whatever vegetables you have lying around. If you can't find barley, use rice, pasta, or potatoes. I like to serve it with homemade croutons topped with some melted blue cheese.

ELK FAJITAS

1 pound elk tenderloin, trimmed and
cut into strips
5 tablespoons extra-virgin olive oil
1 garlic clove, minced
1/4 cup cilantro, minced
Pinch of oregano
Salt and pepper to taste
1 yellow onion,
thinly sliced
4 bell peppers (a mix of red, yellow
and green), cut into thin strips
1 jalapeño chile, cut into thin strips
8 (10-inch) flour tortillas
Good-quality salsa
2 lemons, sliced into wedges

Serves 4

In a medium bowl, mix the elk strips with 2 tablespoons of the olive oil, garlic, cilantro, oregano, salt and pepper. You may store this ahead or set aside for immediate preparation.

Heat the remaining olive oil in a heavy cast-iron skillet. Add the onion and sauté for about 2 minutes. Add the bell peppers and jalapeño chile. Sauté until the vegetables become tender and begin to carmelize. Remove vegetables from pan and keep warm.

Return pan to heat. Add elk and quickly sauté until about medium-rare, adding oil if needed. Do not overcook.

Remove elk from pan when medium-rare or medium. Divide among warmed flour tortillas and top each with the pepper mix. Serve topped with a great salsa and fresh lemon wedges. Enjoy!

LMF

ELK STEAK SALAD

8 ounces elk steaks, prepared
medium-rare, sliced into strips
1/2 cup mushrooms, sliced
1/2 red onion, sliced
1/2 avocado, diced
1/2 cup mandarin orange sections
1/2 red or yellow bell pepper, diced
1 head red leaf lettuce, torn into
bite-size pieces
Italian dressing or balsamic vinegar
and extra-virgin olive oil
Freshly ground pepper to taste

Serves 4

In a large salad bowl, toss all ingredients together. Serve with a nice piece of toasted rustic bread.

LMF

 his is a great dish for leftover elk steaks, if there are any. It also adds texture and great flavor to a spring or summer salad with all the season's colorful produce. This is how I sometimes prepare this, but please adjust the produce to your liking!

ELK MEDALLIONS WITH ROASTED SHALLOTS AND BALSAMIC REDUCTION

4 (4- to 6-ounce) elk medallions
Extra-virgin olive oil
Freshly ground pepper and salt
to taste
4 shallots, peeled and quartered
1 cup balsamic vinegar
1 tablespoon finely chopped Italian
flat-leaf parsley

Serves 2

Rub elk medallions with 1 tablespoon extra-virgin olive oil. Season elk with salt and pepper and set aside. Preheat the grill.

Place shallots in a small saucepan and add enough extra-virgin olive oil to cover the shallots. Bring to a light simmer and cook until tender and just lightly golden brown. Remove from heat and keep warm.

Pour vinegar into another small saucepan and heat over medium-high heat. When vinegar comes to a light simmer, pay close attention and remove from heat as soon as it is reduced by about half. Reserve.

Place elk medallions on the grill when it is nice and hot. Grill meat just until medium-rare. Overcooking the meat will cause it to become dry and tough.

Place medallions on a plate and top with shallots. Drizzle with small droplets of the vinegar and garnish by sprinkling with chopped parsley.

Every bite will be contrasting, interesting, and simply delicious!

LMF

This recipe works well with either elk or venison. If you are caught without any game but are still tempted to try this recipe, I recommend substituting with a thick rib-eye steak. This recipe is quick and simple. The trick to making a simple dish extraordinary is to use extraordinary ingredients. When you have tasty elk or venison, be choosy about your choices you cook with. I use Corfino (a perfect extra-virgin olive oil for game cooking), fragrant balsamic vinegar, and the freshest herbs and shallots available. Of course, freshly ground pepper always makes a difference when seasoning your meat as well. Enjoy!

ELK CHILE COLORADO

6 to 8 New Mexico dried chiles,
washed and stems removed
2 1/2 cups water
Vegetable oil
2 pounds elk meat, cut into
1-inch cubes
1 large onion, chopped
2 Anaheim chiles, chopped
6 garlic cloves, minced
1 (28-ounce) can tomatoes, diced
2 (7-ounce) cans whole mild green
(Anaheim) chiles, chopped
1/2 teaspoon dried oregano leaves
2 cups beef broth
Salt and pepper to taste
Flour tortillas, warm
Shredded cheese
Salsa
Shredded lettuce

Serves 6

Place New Mexico dried chiles in a small saucepan with the water. Bring to a boil, remove from heat and steep chiles for 30 minutes. Place softened chiles and about 1/2 cup of the liquid in a food processor or blender. Process until smooth, adding additional liquid if necessary to purée. Pass mixture through a strainer to remove seeds and any bits of skin.

Heat oil in a large saucepan over medium-high heat. Add meat and brown evenly. Add onion, 2 Anaheim chiles and garlic and cook until onion is translucent. Add tomatoes, canned chiles, oregano, beef broth and processed New Mexico chiles. Cover and bring to a boil. Reduce heat to low and simmer for 2 hours or until meat is tender. While cooking, make sure that there is always enough liquid to barely cover meat. When done, season to taste with salt and pepper.

To serve, ladle chile into bowls and serve with flour tortillas, cheese, salsa and lettuce on the side. Guests can spoon chile onto tortillas and add desired toppings. Chile may also be eaten out of the bowl.

SFL

Fare Game

WILD BOAR CHILI BEANS

5 tablespoons extra-virgin olive oil
1 red onion, minced
1 garlic clove, minced
3 bell peppers, chopped
1 tablespoon fresh jalapeño chile,
minced (optional)
2 pounds ground wild boar
3 cups crushed tomatoes
3 cups kidney beans, cooked
1/4 cup tomato paste
1 tablespoon chili powder
2 dried bay leaves
Pinch of red pepper flakes
Salt and pepper to taste

Serves 4 to 6

In a large pot, heat 4 tablespoons of the olive oil over medium-high heat. Add onion and sauté until golden brown. Add garlic and sauté about 1 minute. Remove from pot into bowl and set aside.

Return pot to heat and add 1 tablespoon olive oil. Sauté bell peppers and jalapeño chile until tender. Remove from pan and add to bowl with onion.

Return pot to heat and add boar; sauté until brown. Add onion mixture, 5 cups water and remaining ingredients. Lower heat to simmer. You may need to add a little more water to make sure mixture is submerged in liquid. Let simmer for at least 1 hour on low. Serve with a homemade skillet corn bread and you've got a meal to remember.

You may substitute lean bulk pork sausage or lean pork cut into 1/2-inch cubes for the wild boar.

STUFFED BELL PEPPERS WITH GROUND BISON

3 tablespoons extra-virgin olive oil
1 small yellow onion, diced
2 garlic cloves, minced
2 pounds ground bison meat
2 tablespoons tomato paste
1 cup dried Italian bread crumbs
1/2 cup milk
2 eggs
Salt and pepper to taste
6 green bell peppers

Serves 6

In a medium sauté pan, heat the olive oil. Add onion and sauté for about 3 minutes, add garlic and sauté about 1 minute. Add bison and tomato paste. Lightly brown. Set aside in a large bowl and cool.

Add remaining ingredients (excluding peppers) to the onion and bison and mix well. Stuff peppers with the mixture. Place in oven and bake at 350 degrees for about 35 to 40 minutes. Garnish the top with parsley.

LMF

THE PERFECT BISON BURGER

Quality mayonnaise
4 good-quality, fresh burger
buns, split
$1^1/3$ pounds ground bison,
ground elk or ground venison,
divided into $1/3$-pound patties
Seasoned salt, kosher salt and freshly
ground pepper to taste
4 slices Pepper Jack cheese (or your
desired cheese)
4 to 8 fresh red leaf lettuce leaves
4 to 8 slices your favorite pickles
4 to 8 thick slices sweet red onion

Serves 4

Preheat the grill. Spread a thin and light layer of mayonnaise on both sides of each burger bun. Place onto a hot griddle or over the grill to toast. Be careful not to burn. When each bun is golden brown, remove and set aside.

Season the burger patties to your desire with seasoned salt, a pinch of kosher salt and freshly ground pepper. Be sure to season both sides of the patties. Grill just until medium-rare to medium. Just before removing from grill, flip burgers over and lay a slice of cheese over each patty. Let melt over the tops and remove burgers. Place on bottom of toasted buns. Top with 1 or 2 lettuce leaves, 1 or 2 pickle slices, or 2 onion slices and bun top. Serve with stone-groud mustard, quality mayonnaise and quality ketchup.

LMF

The key to making a perfect burger is to utilize the freshest and highest quality ingredients available. If you have properly stored your game in a vacuum-sealed package, you should have the first quality ingredient that goes into preparing a spectacular summer meal.

Take a little time and choose fresh, crispy lettuce, a flavorful fresh bun, a juicy tangy pickle, and a thick slice of sweet red onion. Whether you are preparing burgers in your backyard or at camp, everyone is going to think you've made a truly gourmet burger! Remember not to overcook!

Fare Game

BISON TENDERLOIN WITH BASIL PESTO FILLING

1 bison tenderloin, well trimmed
1 cup Pesto Sauce (below)
2 tablespoons extra-virgin olive oil
Salt and pepper to taste

Serve 4 to 6

To prepare the tenderloin, lay out on a cutting board. With a sharp knife, make an incision and slowly roll tenderloin away to cut open like a jelly roll.

When tenderloin is laid out flat, spoon pesto sauce in a thin layer up to 1 inch away from edges. Gently roll back up to original form. Cut butcher's string in increments to securely tie up tenderloin for cooking. Gently rub down with olive oil and season with salt and pepper.

Grill until medium rare. Remove string and cut tenderloin into steaks about 1 inch thick to serve.

PESTO SAUCE

1 bunch basil leaves,
washed and dried
2 garlic cloves, peeled
1/4 cup (about) extra-virgin olive oil
1/2 cup (2 ounces) freshly grated
Parmesan cheese
Pinch of salt
1 tablespoon pine nuts (optional)

Place all ingredients in a food processor or blender. Process until smooth and combined.

LMF

This recipe reflects how delicious something simple can be with complementing ingredients. If you have Armanino Farms frozen pesto sauce available in your area, you may use it in place of homemade. Otherwise, make your own pesto sauce. Other commercial brands are often off flavor and will ruin the dish. Be sure to use the best ingredients in all aspects of your recipe to ensure a great result. In other words, don't skimp on the quality!

Freshwater Game Fish

Bass · Catfish · Pike · Salmon

Sturgeon · Trout · Walleye

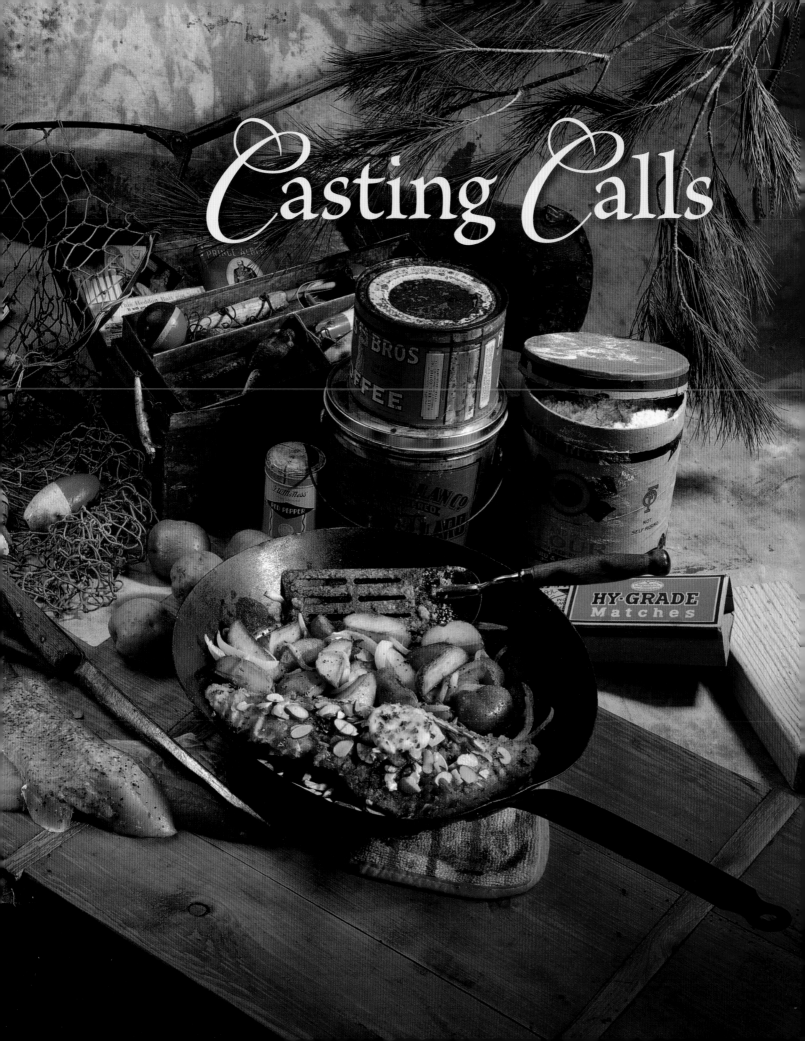

Casting Calls

BASS CROQUETTES

3 garlic cloves, minced
1/2 cup finely chopped onion
1/4 cup finely chopped celery
1/4 cup finely chopped
green pepper
1/2 cup diced tomato
1 tablespoon oil
1/2 teaspoon dried leaf marjoram
1 teaspoon dried dill weed
1/2 teaspoon salt
1/4 teaspoon pepper
2 slices bread, white or wheat
1/2 cup milk
2 tablespoons butter or margarine
2 tablespoons flour
1 cup milk
2 tablespoons Madeira
2 cups chopped bass
1 cup cornmeal

Serves 4

In a large skillet, sauté the garlic, onion, celery, green pepper, and tomato in oil until lightly browned. Add the marjoram, dill, salt and pepper and stir to coat the vegetables. Remove from the heat. In a shallow bowl, combine the bread and 1/2 cup milk and let sit for 10 minutes, until the bread has absorbed the milk. Squeeze the excess milk off the bread, add the bread to the vegetables and mix well together. The milk-soaked bread acts to bind together the croquettes.

To make the white sauce, melt the butter in a small saucepan over medium heat. Add the flour and stir until the mixture is smooth and golden. Slowly add 1 cup milk as you stir, then cook over low heat, stirring for 7 to 10 minutes until the sauce is thick. Pour the sauce into the sautéed vegetables, add the Madeira and fish and stir gently. Spread the mixture out in a shallow baking dish and chill for 60 minutes.

Pour the cornmeal into a shallow bowl and set aside. Once the croquette mixture has chilled, shape it into 1 1/2-inch balls. Lower them carefully into a deep-fat fryer with enough cooking oil to cover at 370 degrees and cook a few at a time for about 3 minutes each, or until crisp and brown. Roll in the cornmeal and serve immediately.

EMC

Here's a great appetizer for your next party: a bite-size, flavor-packed, hot hors d'oeuvre. No need for dipping sauce, either; they stand up quite nicely on their own. Don't be intimidated by the long list of ingredients; You sauté some vegetables, make a simple white sauce, then drop a few fish balls in a deep-fat fryer. It's really quite straightforward.

Casting Calls

CREOLE CORN AND BASS CASSEROLE

1 onion, chopped
5 garlic cloves, minced
1 green bell pepper, chopped
1 tablespoon oil
3 cups frozen corn, thawed
$1/2$ teaspoon salt
$1/4$ teaspoon black pepper
$1/4$ teaspoon cayenne pepper
$1/2$ teaspoon dried oregano leaves
$1/4$ teaspoon dried thyme leaves
$11/2$ pounds bass fillets,
cut into chunks
$1/2$ cup cornmeal
1 egg, slightly beaten
2 cups milk

Serves 4 to 6

Preheat the oven to 350 degrees. In a large skillet, sauté the onion, garlic and green pepper in oil until browned. Add the corn and seasonings and stir well. When the mixture is sizzling again in the pan, stir in the fish chunks and cornmeal. In a small bowl, combine the egg and milk; pour into the pan and stir.

Place in a deep 3-quart casserole and bake, uncovered, for 1 hour.

EMC

This is one of those old-fashioned, one-dish, stick-to-your-ribs meals that seems to be making a comeback in the nether world of urban America. Fortunately, the casserole never really died in the West and Midwest. Just go to any church or community potluck: rich, heavy casseroles are still king of the hill.

Fishing was the most popular recreational activity after
hunting among *Ducks Unlimited*® readers.

SPICY CAJUN FISH FRY

Corn flour
Garlic powder
Onion powder
Cayenne pepper
Salt
Pinch of ground black pepper
1 egg
1¹/2 cups milk
Vegetable oil for frying
1 pound fish (such as halibut,
bass or sturgeon), cut into
1-inch chunks

Serves 2

In a medium bowl, combine corn flour, garlic powder, onion powder, cayenne pepper, salt and black pepper. Mix together well. In another medium bowl, combine the egg and milk and mix together well to make a batter. Heat the oil in a deep fryer or deep pot to 350 degrees.

Dredge the fish chunks in the corn flour mixture. Shake off excess flour. Then dip into the batter; transfer into the hot oil to fry. Turn the fish over with a fork if necessary for even cooking. Cook until evenly golden brown on all sides. Remove the fish from oil and place on several sheets of paper towels to drain. Serve hot with fresh lemon wedges. You may need to adjust seasoning by sprinkling with more spicy seasonings if you desire.

CROSS SEAFOOD CHOWDER

2 onions, chopped
1 rib celery, chopped
¹/2 green bell pepper, chopped
¹/2 cup (1 stick) butter
8 ounces cream cheese, cut into
small pieces
2 (10-ounce) cans cream of
potato soup
2 (10-ounce) cans baby clams
2 (4-ounce) cans small shrimp
2 (6-ounce) cans white crab meat
3 (5-ounce) catfish fillets, chopped
6 cups half-and-half
¹/2 carrot, finely chopped
Dash each of white pepper and salt

Serves 15

Sauté the onions, celery and bell pepper in butter in a stockpot over medium-high heat. Add the cream cheese, soup, clams, shrimp, crab meat, catfish, half-and-half, 1¹/4 cups water and carrot and mix well. Simmer over low heat for 30 minutes. Do not allow to boil. Add the pepper and salt. Serve hot.

Casting Calls

BEER BATTER FISH

2 pounds fish fillets
(halibut, striper, etc.)
Flour for dredging
Pinch of kosher salt
1 cup flour
Pinch of cayenne pepper
(or favorite spicy seasoning)
8 ounces good ale
1 package dry yeast
Vegetable or canola oil for frying

Serves 4

Cut fillets into chunks and dredge in a mixture of flour and salt. Shake off any excess flour.

In a separate bowl, combine 1 cup flour and cayenne pepper; slowly add the beer and yeast. Mix well until of a batter consistency. Dip the floured fillet chunks into the batter and place in 375-degree oil, turning occasionally while cooking. When golden brown and cooked, remove fish from pan and drain on paper towels.

Serve with icy cold beer, fresh lemon wedges and if need be, tartar sauce.

Note: This recipe also makes great tacos! Serve with a cilantro chipotle sour cream sauce.

LMF

FISH POPPERS

18 fresh jalapeño chiles or small
sweet peppers
1 cup cooked fish, broken into pieces
2 green onions, minced
2 tablespoons fresh basil, chopped
1 garlic clove, minced
1 teaspoon lime zest, minced
1 cup (4 ounces) shredded
Pepper Jack cheese
4 ounces cream cheese,
room temperature
1/4 cup seasoned bread crumbs

Serves 6 appetizers

Split peppers lengthwise and place on a baking sheet. Bake in a preheated 400-degree oven for 8 to 10 minutes or until peppers soften. Remove from oven and allow to cool. Carefully scrape out seeds. In a bowl, combine remaining ingredients. Stuff into peppers. Peppers can be broiled or grilled until stuffing is warm.

SFL

RED PEPPER AND CATFISH SOUP

1 onion, chopped
4 ounces mushrooms, sliced
(about 1 1/2 cups)
2 large red bell peppers, sliced
1 ripe tomato, sliced
1 pound catfish fillets, cut into
chunks
2 tablespoons oil
2 cups fish stock or
chicken broth
2 potatoes, peeled and sliced thin
1/2 cup whipping cream
1/4 teaspoon salt
1/4 teaspoon red pepper flakes

Serves 4

In a medium pot, sauté the onion, mushrooms, peppers, tomato and fish chunks in oil until the onion and peppers are tender, about 10 minutes. Add the fish stock and potatoes and bring to a boil. Reduce the heat and simmer, uncovered, for 15 minutes, until the potato slices break up easily when stirred.

Remove the soup from the heat and let cool for about 15 minutes or until it is safe to put in the food processor or blender. Purée the soup and return it to the pot.

Bring the soup back to a simmer. Add the cream, salt, and pepper flakes (add more, to taste) and serve immediately, with hard rolls and a grating of Parmesan cheese, if desired.

EMC

You can use any white-fleshed fish for this soup; I just happened to have a bunch of catfish fillets in the freezer. With the fish, potatoes, and peppers, it's a complete meal, and one that will warm up anybody on a cold, rainy day.

BLACKENED CATFISH

Blackening Seasoning

2 teaspoons paprika
1/4 teaspoon basil leaves
1/4 teaspoon ground oregano
1/4 teaspoon thyme
1/4 teaspoon ground black pepper
1/2 teaspoon onion powder
1/2 teaspoon garlic powder
1/2 teaspoon white pepper
1/2 teaspoon cayenne pepper
3 teaspoon salt

Catfish

4 catfish fillets, 6 to 8 ounces each
2 tablespoons olive oil
2 tablespoons bacon grease
1/4 cup sour cream
2 teaspoons lime juice
Pinch of sugar

Serves 4

The Seasoning: Combine blackening seasoning ingredients in a bowl and mix well.

The Catfish: Rub fish with olive oil and then coat evenly with spice mixture. Cover and refrigerate for 30 to 60 minutes. Heat bacon grease in a heavy skillet, preferably cast-iron, over high heat. Add fish and sear on one side until blackened. Flip over and sear the other side, but just until fish is cooked and not overcooked. Place fish on plates, blackest side up. Combine sour cream, lime juice and sugar and spoon over fish.

SFL

atfish has a fairly high fat content, and it's even better with bacon grease—but then, aren't most recipes? It's best to prepare this one outdoors. Whenever you pepper-coat something and burn it in a pan, it will create fumes that make it difficult to breathe when you're in close quarters. Add to that a mess of splattering bacon grease, and you've got trouble. If you decide to cook it indoors, open the windows, rank up the fans, and be listening for the smoke detector alarm. It might be a good time to check the batteries! This recipe is best with thick fillets from large catfish. You can substitute commercial blackening seasoning or Cajun spice. If you make your own and are missing an ingredient or two, nobody will notice.

CATFISH WRAP WITH AVOCADO AND TOMATO SALSA

Avocado and Tomato Salsa
2 ripe but firm avocados, diced
2 limes, juice only
1 cup cherry or pear tomatoes, halved and drained (toss gently in a colander)
1/4 cup red onion, minced
2 garlic cloves, minced
3 tablespoons fresh cilantro leaves, chopped
2 tablespoons olive oil
Salt and pepper to taste

Wraps
1 1/2 pounds catfish fillets
2 tablespoons olive oil
1 tablespoon lemon pepper
1 lemon, juice only
1 lime, juice only
4 large warm flour tortillas
2 cups prepared coleslaw (I like the creamy kind)
Hot sauce, Tabasco sauce, etc.
1 cup (4 ounces) mixed shredded Cheddar and Pepper Jack cheese

Serves 4

The Salsa: Combine the avocados, lime juice, tomatoes, onion, garlic, cilantro, salt and pepper in a bowl and toss gently.

The Wraps: Rub fish with olive oil and lemon pepper. Grill or cook in a hot, well-oiled pan just until done. While cooking, squeeze lemon and lime juice over fish.

Lay a warm tortilla on a work surface and put cooked fish along the bottom third of the tortilla, leaving about 2 inches of space between the fish and the bottom edge of the tortilla. Stuffing ingredients must be flat, not mounded. Spoon some coleslaw onto the fish, add a dash or two of hot sauce and top with cheese. Spoon some of the salsa onto the cheese. Fold the bottom edge over the stuffing and fold one of the sides over toward the center to keep the stuffing from falling out. Continue rolling snugly from the bottom and serve with additional salsa on the side.

How you cook the fish is your call, but I prefer the smoky flavor of grilled fish. However you decide to cook it, just don't cook it too long! The coleslaw makes it cool, creamy, and crunchy. The biggest tortillas you can find work best. If all you can locate are smaller ones, allow two per person and go easy on the stuffing.

Current membership exceeds 650,000 members, making Ducks Unlimited® one of the most active grassroots, volunteer-based organizations in the outdoors and conservation community.

Casting Calls

PIKE PUFFS

1/2 small onion, finely diced
1/2 cup mayonnaise
5 tablespoons grated
Parmesan cheese
2 tablespoons finely chopped
fresh parsley
1/2 teaspoon dried leaf tarragon
1/4 teaspoon salt
1/4 teaspoon pepper
8 ounces cooked pike, flaked
5 or 6 slices white bread

Serves 8 to 10 as appetizers

Preheat oven to 350 degrees. In a medium bowl, combine the onion, mayonnaise and 3 tablespoons of the Parmesan cheese with the parsley, tarragon, salt and pepper. Mix thoroughly, then fold in the pike bits. Cover and refrigerate while you prepare the toast rounds.

Remove the crusts from the bread and cut each slice into 9 squares. Place on a cookie sheet and bake until lightly golden on one side, about 10 minutes. Remove the cookie sheet from the oven and preheat the broiler. Be sure the rack is about 6 inches away from the heat source for the broiling.

Spread 1 teaspoon of the pike mixture on each toast square. Return the squares to the cookie sheet, sprinkle with the remaining Parmesan cheese and brown lightly under the broiler. Serve hot.

EMC

Need an easy-to-make appetizer for your New Year's Day family get-together? Or maybe you need to impress the boss, new in-laws, or just plain give yourself a treat. Try these cheesy, rich-tasting puffs. And if you don't have any pike in the freezer, feel free to experiment. Depending on your tastes, anything—including salmon bits—could fill this bill.

Maybe Next Time
Ralph J. McDonald

International Artist of the Year
—1981, 2006

R.J. McDonald is one of our country's most highly respected wildlife artists. For more than twenty-five years his paintings and prints have been eagerly collected by knowledgeable art enthusiasts. Over the years Ralph, as his friends call him, has made numerous contributions to conservation groups. Among these groups are Ducks Unlimited®, Game Conservation International, Deer Unlimited, and The National Wild Turkey Federation. In 1981 Ducks Unlimited® named him its National Artist of the Year for *Black Magic at Little Lake*, and the sales of his prints at DU™ auctions have raised millions of dollars for that organization. Recently Ducks Unlimited® and the National Wild Turkey Federation each selected a McDonald painting to publish as a print for their national fund-raising projects.

LEMON-LIME SMOKED SALMON DIP

8 ounces smoked salmon
8 ounces cream cheese, softened
1 tablespoon freshly chopped dill
2 tablespoons fresh lemon juice
1/4 teaspoon coarse black pepper
Few dashes of Tabasco sauce
(or your favorite hot sauce)
Pinch of salt

Serves 4

In a food processor, mix all ingredients and blend until combined and smooth. Garnish the top with a sprig of fresh dill. Serve with your favorite crackers or a good crusty rustic bread.

LMF

FRESH SALMON WITH HERB AND CAPER BUTTER

4 (6-ounce) fresh salmon fillets
Olive oil
Salt to taste
Pinch of white pepper
1 pound (4 sticks) unsalted butter, softened
Kosher salt to taste
1 to 2 tablespoons capers
1 tablespoon freshly minced dill
Couple dashes of Tabasco sauce

Serves 4

Baste filets with olive oil, salt and white pepper. Grill, pan-sear or broil just until cooked through.

Combine remaining ingredients together in a food processor or in a mixing bowl. Roll into a tube that is about 1 1/2 inches wide. Wrap in foil and chill in refrigerator for future use. Slice just before serving and serve over hot salmon.

May adjust seasonings with your favorite herbs and seasonings.

LMF

Ducks Unlimited® ranks 105 out of more than 1,000,000 nonprofit organizations in the United States based on budget size.

GRILLED SALMON WITH AVOCADO AND CUCUMBER SALSA

Grilled Salmon
3 tablespoons olive oil
2 tablespoons lemon juice
3 garlic cloves, minced
Salt and pepper to taste
4 salmon fillets

Avocado and Cucumber Salsa
1 1/2 cups cucumbers, peeled, seeded
and diced into 1/4-inch cubes
1/3 cup red onion, finely diced
1 jalapeño chile, seeded
and minced
3 garlic cloves, minced
1/2 cup tomato, seeded and diced
(or halved cherry tomatoes)
1 tablespoon freshly squeezed
lime juice
1/2 teaspoon red pepper flakes
1/2 teaspoon sugar
1/4 cup seasoned rice vinegar
1/4 cup fresh cilantro leaves,
roughly chopped
3 tablespoons olive oil
1 cup fresh avocado, cut into
1/2-inch pieces

4 servings

The Salmon: In a small bowl, combine olive oil, lemon juice and garlic. Add some salt and pepper and rub mixture over fillets. Cover and refrigerate for 1 to 2 hours. Grill on a hot grill for 3 to 4 minutes per side or just until cooked, but not overcooked.

The Salsa: Combine the salsa ingredients in a bowl. Let stand at room temperature for 30 minutes to allow the flavors to blend. Serve over the grilled salmon.

SFL

This one is best cooked on a smoky grill, but you can broil or pan-sear the salmon if you prefer. The salsa has a mixture of textures from smooth and creamy to crunchy. If you make enough of it, it can serve as your salad course.

STURGEON WITH BRANDY ORANGE SAUCE

4 (6-ounce) sturgeon steaks
Salt and pepper to taste
1 tablespoon olive oil
1 tablespoon butter
1/4 cup brandy
1/2 teaspoon fresh ginger, grated
1/2 cup freshly squeezed orange juice
1 lemon, juice only
1 lime, juice only
1/4 cup dried nectarines, peaches
or apricots
1/4 cup dried cherries or cranberries
(Craisins work fine)
2 tablespoons cold butter

Serves 4

Season fish with salt and pepper. Heat olive oil and 1 tablespoon butter in a skillet over medium-high heat. Add fish to pan and sear on one side, about 3 minutes. Flip fish over and sear 2 minutes. Add brandy and ginger to the pan. BUT FIRST . . .

Caution—Danger—Watch It—Look Out—Don't put your face anywhere near the pan when you add brandy. It will probably flame up and burn something, like your face, the drapes, etc. Check the area around the pan before adding any alcohol.

OK, anyone who burns something now was not paying attention. You can reduce the risk of flames by combining the brandy with the fruit juices and adding slowly to the pan. Or . . . after adding the brandy, let the flames subside and then add orange, lemon and lime juices. Add dried fruits. Remove fish and keep warm. It's done. Reduce liquid to 1/4 cup. Stir in 2 tablespoons butter until melted. Season with salt and pepper.

To serve, place sturgeon on plate and spoon sauce over the top.

S_{FL}

Sturgeon ranks near the top of my list of favorite fish. The flavor and texture is unlike any other fish. It is firm to the bite and somewhat neutral in flavor. The texture is reminiscent of a cross between pork and fish. As an added bonus, there are no bones to mess with—just the cartilage. Filleting is a snap, and you can grill, pan-sear, broil or sauté this strange-looking creature. It looks prehistoric. It tastes out of this world.

Casting Calls

MARINATED AND GRILLED STURGEON

1/2 cup extra-virgin olive oil
2 tablespoons fresh dill, finely chopped
1 tablespoon minced shallot
Pinch of crushed red pepper flakes
Salt and freshly ground pepper to taste
2 (4- to 6-ounce) sturgeon fillets
Lemon wedges (optional)

Serves 2

Mix the first 6 ingredients in a bowl. Add sturgeon fillets, (be sure to completely coat the fillets), cover and refrigerate for at least 2 hours. When coals are ready, place onto grill. Cook for about 4 minutes on each side or until firm and cooked to desired doneness. Squeeze fresh lemon juice over fish while grilling to enhance the fruitiness of the flavor.

Note: Replace the dill with fresh cilantro and you have a start to a great fish taco recipe.

LMF

This is a great fish for grilling. The texture is excellent and when cooked fresh, the simplest ingredients make it an outstanding dish!

TROUT WITH CREAMY DILL SAUCE

2 trout fillets
1 cup flour
Salt and pepper to taste
3 tablespoons olive oil
Juice of 1/2 lemon
Splash of chardonnay
1 tablespoon butter
1/3 cup sour cream
1 tablespoon freshly chopped dill

Serves 2

Dredge the trout in flour and shake off excess. Season with salt and pepper. Heat olive oil in skillet over medium-high heat. Lay trout in the skillet flesh side down and cook until golden brown; turn over to finish cooking process. When fish is cooked but still firm, remove from skillet and keep warm. Add the wine to the skillet to reduce a bit; add the lemon juice. Give it about a minute or so to reduce about half the liquid. Stir in the sour cream and dill. Remove pan from heat. Stir in the butter until smooth. Pour sauce over trout and serve with a lemon wedge.

LMF

This is a quick, easy, great way to make a gourmet meal out of your fresh catch at the campfire.

PAN-FRIED TROUT WITH SIMPLE HERB SAUCE

1 large trout, cut into fillets
1 cup flour
3 tablespoons extra-virgin olive oil
Salt and pepper to taste
Splash of sauvignon blanc or other white wine
Juice of 1/2 lemon
3 tablespoons fresh Italian flat-leaf parsley, finely chopped
1 tablespoon fresh dill, finely chopped
1 or 2 tablespoons butter

Serves 1 or 2

Dredge trout fillets in flour. Shake off excess. Heat olive oil in a medium sauté pan over medium-high heat. Season the trout fillets with salt and pepper. Place in sauté pan and cook until golden brown on both sides, about 7 to 8 minutes total. Cooking time will vary depending on the size of your trout. You want the fish to just start flaking but not fall apart. Remove fish from pan and set aside.

Deglaze pan with wine. Add lemon juice and herbs. Sauté about 1 minute; you just want to cook the herbs long enough to release their aromatic oils, but be careful not to burn them. Remove from heat and swirl in butter. Pour over golden trout and serve. Quick, simple and memorable!

Note: Dried herbs may be substituted if fresh are not available. Reduce amount by half.

STUFFED TROUT

1 trout, left whole with head on
2 tablespoons extra-virgin olive oil
Salt and pepper to taste
3 sprigs of fresh dill (or 1 tablespoon dried)
1 orange, sliced
1 lemon, sliced
Butter (optional)

Serves 1 or 2

Lay trout in the center of a large piece of foil. Rub all over with the oil. Season with salt and pepper. Stuff with dill; top the dill with the lemon and orange. Layer with butter. Wrap up the trout in the foil as if it were a small package so that juice will not drip out. You may cook this on a grill, turning once, or cook in oven at 375 degrees for about 18 minutes. Be sure to pour the juices from the foil onto the servings.

Wrap up this recipe and forget about messing with it until it is done. If you're not counting calories, go ahead and throw in a couple tablespoons of butter before wrapping up the fish to cook. It will give it just a touch of richness. The cooked juices will serve as its own sauce.

GRILLED MARINATED TROUT

1/3 cup red wine vinegar
1/3 cup orange juice
3 garlic cloves, minced
3 green onions, minced
1/3 cup tomato, seeded and
finely diced
1 tablespoon capers, rinsed and
chopped
1/2 teaspoon kosher salt
1/4 teaspoon freshly ground
black pepper
1 cup olive oil
4 (1-pound) trout, rinsed and
patted dry (or the equivalent
in larger fish)

Serves 4

In a medium bowl, combine vinegar and next 7 ingredients. Add olive oil in a thin stream while whisking vigorously to emulsify. Place trout in a plastic or glass container and pour half the mixture over. Reserve remaining half to baste fish during grilling. Cover fish and refrigerate for 2 hours, turning every 30 minutes.

Remove fish from marinade and pat dry to avoid flare-ups from marinade while grilling. On a hot, well-lubricated grill, brown fish on one side, about 5 minutes, depending on the size of the fish. Baste fish with reserved marinade while cooking, saving a few tablespoons of the marinade to drizzle over cooked fish when served.

Note: If your fish tends to stick to the grill, you're not alone. To avoid fish stickage, make sure that your grill is clean, well-oiled and hot before placing any fish on the grates. If you rub your fish with some decent olive oil, it'll improve the flavor and help keep it from sticking.

SFL

WALLEYE FRITTERS CARIBBEAN STYLE

8 ounces walleye chunks

1/4 cup chopped green onions

1/4 cup chopped fresh parsley

1 teaspoon dried thyme leaf

3 garlic cloves, minced

1 scotch bonnet or habanero chile, seeded and minced

1 cup milk

1 1/3 cups flour

1 egg, lightly beaten

Peanut or canola oil for frying

1 teaspoon salt

1 lime, cut into wedges

4 servings

In a large bowl, combine the walleye with the green onions, parsley, thyme, garlic and chile and mix well. In a separate bowl, combine the milk, flour and egg and stir just until smooth. Gently stir the milk mixture into the fish mixture.

Fill the deep-fat fryer with peanut or canola oil to the manufacturer's suggested level, then preheat to 375 degrees. When the oil is hot, test it by dropping 1 tablespoon of the batter into the oil. The fritter should be deep brown in 3 to 4 minutes. After you test, you can cook several tablespoon-sized fritters at the same time—just be sure they float freely and are not crowded together. Remove the fritters from the fryer and sprinkle lightly with salt as they drain on a paper towel. Serve hot with a squeeze of lime.

Note: If all you can find is a dried chile, let it soak 15 to 20 minutes in a bit of the milk to soften, then purée in a blender. If using fresh chile, it is the seeds and white inner ribbing that hold a lot of the heat. If you are not into hot stuff, be sure to remove both before cooking—using rubber gloves to handle all hot peppers. Heat seekers are on their own.

EMC

When you're done filleting your catch, there's still a good bit of meat on the bones you don't want to waste. But what can you do with those little chunks? Gumbo, chowder, fish balls, fish cakes are a few options. But if you have a hunger for hot stuff, you owe it to yourself to try this Caribbean twist: the scotch bonnet chile. Scotch bonnet may not sound like much, but it packs a wallop that is more cumulative than immediate. A word to the wise? If you can't find these Caribbean chiles, try habanero or another hi-octane variety. And use rubber gloves when you handle them—dried or fresh, the active ingredients may stay active on your fingers for several days.

Casting Calls

SIMPLE WALLEYE SALAD SANDWICHES

1 pound walleye fillets
1 cup mayonnaise
1/2 teaspoon garlic powder
1 tablespoon green Tabasco sauce
2 cucumbers, peeled and diced
1 cup finely chopped onion
3/4 cup finely chopped red
bell pepper
4 to 6 deli rolls, split, or
8 to 12 slices wheat bread
3 tomatoes, sliced
Lettuce
Slices of sweet Vidalia onions

Serves 4 to 6

Lay the walleye fillets in a single layer on paper towels or on a plate in the microwave and cook until they are still moist but fall apart when you try to pick them up, about 1 1/2 to 2 minutes in a 500-watt unit; 1 minute in a 700-watt microwave. Or you can bake them in a 350-degree oven for 10 minutes. Chill 1 to 3 hours.

In a medium bowl, combine the mayonnaise, garlic powder and Tabasco sauce and stir well. Add the cucumbers, chopped onion and red pepper and toss. Finally, break the chilled fillets into small pieces and fold them into the mayonnaise mixture.

To serve, pile the walleye salad on half a deli roll. Top with tomato, lettuce, thinly sliced onion and the other half of the roll.

EMC

Tired of buying cans of tuna fish when you've got a freezer full of better tasting fish? Here's a simple way to make a delicious tuna salad substitute— if you want to call something that tastes better than the original a substitute.

Wild Sides & Sweet Endings
Vegetables & Side Dishes · Desserts

After the Hunt

SUGARED ASPARAGUS

3 tablespoons butter or margarine
2 tablespoons brown sugar
2 pounds fresh asparagus, cut into
1-inch pieces
1 cup chicken broth

Serves 4 to 6

Melt the butter in a skillet over medium-high heat. Add the brown sugar and cook until it dissolves. Add the asparagus and sauté for 2 minutes. Stir in the broth. Bring to a boil; reduce the heat, cover and simmer for 8 to 10 minutes or until the asparagus is tender-crisp. Transfer the asparagus to a serving dish and keep warm. Cook the sauce until it is reduced by half. Pour over the asparagus and serve immediately.

ITALIAN GREEN BEANS

3 tablespoons olive oil
1 onion, chopped
4 garlic cloves, chopped
5 large tomatoes, chopped
3/4 cup dry white wine
1 pound green beans, cooked and
drained
1/2 cup sliced back olives
1 1/2 teaspoons lemon juice
Salt and pepper to taste

Serves 4

Heat the oil in a deep skillet over medium heat. Add the onion and garlic and cook until tender. Add the tomatoes and wine and cook for 15 minutes, stirring occasionally. Add the beans and olives and cook until heated through. Add the lemon juice, salt and pepper; stir to combine.

Wild Sides & Sweet Endings

GLAZED BABY CARROTS

2 pounds baby carrots,
peeled and trimmed
2 tablespoons lightly salted butter
2 tablespoons honey
Kosher salt to taste
Freshly ground pepper to taste
1/4 cup ginger ale

Serves 6

Sauté the carrots in the butter in a saucepan for 1 minute. Add the honey, salt and pepper and toss to coat well. Stir in the ginger ale gently. Bring to a boil. Reduce the heat and simmer, covered, for 3 minutes. Simmer, uncovered, for 5 minutes or until the carrots are tender and evenly glazed.

SCALLOPED CORN

1 onion, chopped
1 cup chopped green bell pepper
1/4 cup (1/2 stick) butter or margarine
1 (15-ounce) can cream-style corn
1 (15-ounce) can whole kernel
corn, drained
1 (7- to 8-ounce) package (no egg
added) corn bread mix
1 cup sour cream
1 1/2 cups (6 ounces) shredded
Cheddar cheese

Serves 6

Preheat the oven to 350 degrees. Sauté the onion and bell pepper in the butter in a saucepan until tender. Add the corn and corn bread mix and mix well. Stir in the sour cream and 1 cup of the cheese. Spoon into a greased 6-cup square baking dish. Sprinkle with the remaining 1/2 cup cheese. Bake for 40 minutes or until golden brown and set.

Ducks Unlimited® consistently ranks among the top five private gun buyers in the United States. During the past five years, Ducks Unlimited® has sold an average of 15,000 guns annually at fund-raising events nationwide. Proceeds from the sale of these guns raised approximately $6.7 million each year for wetland conservation.

GRILLED CORN ON THE COB WITH JALAPEÑO LIME BUTTER

6 ears unhusked sweet corn
1 small fresh jalapeño chile
1 garlic clove
1/2 cup (1 stick) butter or margarine, softened
Grated zest of 1 lime
1/4 teaspoon paprika
1/2 teaspoon chili powder

Serves 6

Soak the unhusked corn in water to cover for 2 hours. Cut the jalapeño into halves and discard the seeds. Combine with the garlic in a food processor container. Process until finely minced. Add the butter, lime zest, paprika and chili powder and blend well.

Preheat the grill. Peel back the husks from the cob without removing them. Remove the corn silk. Brush the corn with jalapeño lime butter. Rewrap the cobs with the husks. Secure at the end with wet twine or thin wire. Grill over the hot coals for 30 minutes, turning occasionally. Serve with the remaining jalapeño lime butter.

GRILLED SWEET BELLS

1 red and 1 yellow bell pepper
2 cups fresh salsa
8 ounces shredded Monterey Jack cheese

Serves 4

Preheat the grill to medium-high heat. Cut the peppers in half lengthwise, then again lengthwise through the spine forming a cup to hold the filling. Remove the seeds.

Divide the salsa among the pepper cups, then top with the cheese. Grill until the pepper looks a bit charred on bottom and the cheese is melted, about 20 minutes. Transfer to a serving platter with tongs and serve hot.

Red bell peppers are just old standby green bell peppers that have been allowed to ripen a bit longer on the vine, which makes them much sweeter.

Wild Sides & Sweet Endings

Parmesan Scalloped Potatoes

3/4 cup (3 ounces) freshly grated
Parmesan cheese
3 tablespoons chopped fresh
marjoram, or 1 tablespoon dried
1 teaspoon salt
3/4 teaspoon garlic powder
1/4 teaspoon coarsely ground pepper
1/4 teaspoon ground nutmeg
5 large baking potatoes, peeled and
thinly sliced
3 cups whipping cream
3/4 cup water
3 tablespoons freshly grated
Parmesan cheese
1 1/2 tablespoons chopped fresh
marjoram, or 1 1/2 teaspoons dried

Serves 8

Preheat the oven to 350 degrees. Combine 3/4 cup cheese, 3 tablespoons fresh marjoram, the salt, garlic powder, pepper and nutmeg in a small bowl.

Layer 1/3 of the potatoes and half of the cheese mixture in a lightly greased shallow 3-quart baking dish. Repeat the layers; top with the remaining potatoes.

Combine the whipping cream and water in a small bowl. Pour over the potatoes. Sprinkle with 3 tablespoons cheese and 1 1/2 tablespoons fresh marjoram. Bake, covered, for 1 1/2 hours. Bake, uncovered, for 30 minutes longer or until the potatoes are tender. Let stand for 10 minutes before serving.

Fancy Mashed Potatoes

6 large potatoes, peeled and chopped
2 (8-ounce) containers green
onion dip
6 ounces cream cheese, softened
1/2 cup (1 stick) butter or margarine
1 teaspoon garlic salt
1/4 cup (about) milk
Paprika to taste

Serves 8

Preheat oven to 350 degrees. Cook potatoes in water to cover in saucepan for 15 minutes or until tender; drain. Mash potatoes in a mixing bowl. Add onion dip, cream cheese, butter and garlic salt, beating until smooth. Add enough milk 1 tablespoon at a time to make of desired consistency. Spoon into 1 1/2-quart baking dish. Sprinkle with paprika. Prepare to this point in advance if desired and bake just before serving time. Bake for 30 minutes. Serve immediately.

Note: You may use 2 (24-ounce) packages frozen mashed potato steamers prepared using package directions for the cooked potatoes. Recipe may be halved.

POTATO PANCAKES

1 (24-ounce) bag frozen
hash browns, thawed
2 eggs
3/4 cup sour cream
1/4 cup flour
1 cup chopped onion
(about 1/2 medium onion)
1 1/2 teaspoons salt
1 teaspoon pepper
1 apple, grated
1/2 teaspoon ground clove
1/4 cup oil or margarine
(or half each)

Makes 12 (4-inch) pancakes

Combine all the ingredients except the oil in a large bowl and stir together. Preheat the oven to 200 degrees and set a plate on the center rack.

Heat 1 to 2 tablespoons butter/oil in a skillet for each batch. Spoon about 1/4 cup batter into the skillet for each pancake and brown the pancakes on both sides over high heat, about 7 minutes. Keep warm in the oven; serve hot.

SPINACH SQUARES

1 cup all-purpose flour
1 cup milk
2 eggs, beaten
1 teaspoon salt
16 ounces Monterey Jack
cheese, shredded
1 (10-ounce) package frozen
chopped spinach, thawed and
squeezed dry
2 tablespoons butter, melted

Serves 8 to 10

Combine the flour, milk, eggs and salt in a large bowl. Mix well. Fold in the cheese and spinach. Brush a 9×12-inch baking dish with the melted butter. Spoon the spinach mixture into the prepared dish. Bake at 375 degrees for 30 minutes. Cool for 5 minutes before cutting into squares.

The dollars raised at local DU™ events are the primary funds that
drive our waterfowl habitat conservation programs.

Wild Sides & Sweet Endings

RESTUFFED SWEET POTATOES

12 small sweet potatoes
Vegetable oil
8 ounces Neufchâtel cheese or
cream cheese, softened
1/4 cup packed light brown sugar
1/4 cup (1/2 stick) butter or margarine
1 to 2 tablespoons sherry
1 1/4 teaspoons salt
1/2 teaspoon pepper
1/3 cup coarsely chopped pecans

Serves 12

Preheat oven to 375 degrees. Prick the sweet potatoes all over with a fork. Rub lightly with oil. Place on a baking sheet. Bake for 1 hour or until tender. Cool slightly. Reduce oven temperature to 350 degrees.

Cut a 1/2-inch strip from the long side of each sweet potato. Scoop out pulp with a spoon, reserving 1/4-inch-thick shells. Beat sweet potato pulp in a mixing bowl until smooth. Add the Neufchâtel cheese, brown sugar, butter, sherry, salt and pepper; mix well. Spoon into the reserved shells. Place on a baking sheet. Sprinkle with the pecans. Bake potatoes for 30 minutes or until heated through.

Note: May spoon filling into a casserole and bake as directed. May prepare and refrigerate for up to 2 days before reheating. Do not eat sweet potato shells.

RICE AND BROCCOLI CASSEROLE

2 cups instant brown rice
2 (10-ounce) cans cream of
chicken soup
2 1/2 cups milk
2 cups (8 ounces) shredded
Cheddar cheese
2 cups sour cream
2 packages frozen broccoli
florets, thawed

Serves 8

Combine the rice, soup and milk in a large bowl. Add the cheese and sour cream and mix well. Fold in the broccoli. Spoon into a greased 9×13-inch baking dish. Bake at 350 degrees for 30 minutes or until the rice is plumped and tender.

Note: This dish may be made ahead before baking and refrigerated for up to 2 days.

HOPPIN' JOHN DRESSING

5 slices bacon
1 onion, chopped
1 (16-ounce) package frozen
black-eyed peas
1 cup water
1 teaspoon salt
2 cups cooked long grain white rice
Dash of hot pepper sauce
1/2 cup chopped green onions
3 tablespoons chopped parsley
Salt and pepper to taste

Serves 6 to 8

Sauté the bacon in a large deep skillet until crisp-cooked. Remove to a paper towel-lined plate using a slotted spoon. Sauté the onion in the bacon drippings in the skillet until tender. Add the black-eyed peas, water and salt and bring to a boil; reduce the heat. Simmer for 20 minutes, stirring occasionally.

Crumble the bacon. Add the bacon, rice, hot pepper sauce, green onions, parsley, salt and pepper to the black-eyed peas. Heat for 3 to 5 minutes. Serve with roasted quail.

Wild Sides & Sweet Endings

APRICOT AND BROWN RICE PILAF

1 cup shredded carrots
1 tablespoon pine nuts
1 tablespoon margarine
3/4 cup quick-cooking brown rice
1 cup apple juice
3/4 cup water
6 dried apricot halves, chopped
2 tablespoons raisins

Serves 4

Combine the carrots, pine nuts and margarine in 1-quart glass dish. Microwave on High for 2 minutes. Add the rice, apple juice and water; mix well. Microwave, loosely covered, on High for 5 minutes, stirring once. Stir in apricots and raisins. Microwave, covered, on Medium for 12 minutes or until liquid is absorbed and rice is tender.

Note: May serve immediately or use as a stuffing.

ZESTY PEPPER RICE

1 teaspoon corn oil
1 red bell pepper, diced
1 green bell pepper, diced
1 cup long grain rice
2 cups water
1/2 teaspoon salt
1/2 cup salsa
1/2 teaspoon dried cilantro or parsley

Serves 4 to 6

Heat the oil in a saucepan over medium heat. Add the bell peppers and sauté for 3 to 4 minutes or until lightly browned. Add the rice, water and salt and bring to a boil. Reduce the heat to low and simmer, covered, for 20 minutes or until the liquid is absorbed. Remove from the heat and add the salsa and cilantro. Let rest, covered, for 5 minutes.

Our local DU™ event system would fail to exist without the dedicated volunteers
who organize and manage local DU™ chapters across the country.

WILD RICE AND MUSHROOM CASSEROLE

3 (6-ounce) packages long grain and
wild rice mix
3 or 4 ribs celery, chopped
4 green onions, chopped
1 green bell pepper, chopped
12 fresh mushrooms, sliced
3/4 cup whipping cream

Serves 10 to 12

Preheat the oven to 350 degrees. Cook the rice using the
package directions. Combine with the celery, onions, bell
pepper and mushrooms in a bowl; mix well. Spoon into a
2-quart baking dish. Pour the whipping cream over the top.
Prepare to this point in advance if desired and bake just
before serving time. Bake for 30 minutes or until bubbly,
stirring several times.

BAKED STUFFING SCOOPS

1/2 cup chopped onion
1 cup chopped celery
1 (16-ounce) can cream-style corn
1/2 cup water
1/4 cup butter or margarine
1 (8-ounce) package corn bread
stuffing mix
2 eggs, beaten
1/4 cup (1/2 stick) butter or
margarine, melted

Serves 8 to 10

Preheat the oven to 350 degrees. Combine the onion, celery,
corn, water and 1/4 cup butter in a saucepan. Bring to a boil
over medium heat. Add the stuffing mix; mix well. Stir in
the eggs. Shape into balls with ice cream scoop; arrange in
9×13-inch baking dish or spoon into a greased 6-cup baking
dish. Drizzle 1/4 cup melted butter over the top. Bake for
30 minutes or until crisp and golden brown. Arrange on a
serving plate.

CROSS CORN BREAD

3 cups self-rising cornmeal
1 cup self-rising flour
2 tablespoons sugar
1 teaspoon baking powder
1 1/2 cups milk
1 egg
2 tablespoons peanut oil

Serves 6 to 8

Combine the cornmeal, flour, sugar, baking powder, milk and egg in a large bowl and mix well. Pour the peanut oil into a 10-inch cast-iron skillet or heavy 9×11-inch baking dish. Heat in a 450-degree oven until hot. Pour the hot oil into the batter and mix well. Pour the batter into the skillet. Bake for 25 to 30 minutes or until golden brown.

BJC

SOUR CREAM MUFFINS

1/4 cup (1/2 stick) butter or margarine, softened
1/4 cup sour cream
1/2 cup buttermilk baking mix or self-rising flour

Makes 1 dozen

Preheat oven to 425 degrees. Combine the butter and sour cream in a bowl; mix well. Stir in the baking mix. Spoon into a greased miniature muffin cups. Bake for 12 to 15 minutes or until golden brown. Serve hot.

EASY BANANA BREAD

2 small bananas, mashed
1¹/2 cups sugar
¹/2 cup vegetable oil
2 eggs, beaten
¹/2 cup milk
1 tablespoon cider vinegar
1 teaspoon baking powder
1¹/2 cups all-purpose flour
1 cup chopped nuts, optional

Serves 8 to 10

Preheat the oven to 350 degrees. Combine the bananas, sugar, oil and eggs in a mixing bowl and mix well. Combine the milk and vinegar in a small bowl and let stand for several minutes. Stir in the baking powder and add to the banana mixture. Stir in the flour and nuts just until moistened. Spoon into a large greased and floured loaf pan or small bundt pan. Bake for 30 minutes or until the bread tests done. Cool in the pan for 10 minutes, then invert onto a wire rack to cool completely.

HERB CHEESE BREAD

2 ounces crumbled blue cheese
1 cup (4 ounces) shredded
Colby-Jack cheese
3 ounces cream cheese, softened
1 tablespoon sherry
1 teaspoon minced garlic
1 tablespoon chopped fresh chives
1 tablespoon chopped fresh parsley
1 (16-ounce) loaf sourdough, French
or Italian bread

Serves 6 to 8

Combine the blue cheese, Colby-Jack cheese, cream cheese, sherry, garlic, chives and parsley in a bowl and mix well. Cut the loaf into 3/4-inch slices without cutting all the way through. Spread the cheese mixture on the cut sides. Wrap the loaf in foil, leaving the ends open. Bake at 375 degrees for 15 to 20 minutes or until the cheese is melted and the bread is toasted. You may also heat the loaf on a grill over medium coals.

Wild Sides & Sweet Endings

OVERNIGHT BAKED APPLES

1/2 cup raisins
1 cup chopped pecans
1 cup packed light brown sugar
8 apples
Cinnamon and nutmeg to taste
2 tablespoons butter or margarine
1/2 cup water

8 servings

Combine the raisins, pecans and brown sugar in a bowl; mix well. Peel the top 1/3 of the apples; remove the cores. Fill with the raisin mixture. Place in a slow-cooker. Sprinkle with the cinnamon and nutmeg; dot with the butter. Pour the water around the apples. Cook on Low for 8 hours to overnight.

PECAN COBBLER

Crust
1 cup sugar
1 cup self-rising flour
1 cup milk
1/2 cup (1 stick) butter, melted

Filling
1 1/2 cups light corn syrup
1 1/2 cups sugar
7 eggs, beaten
1/4 cup (1/2 stick) butter, melted
2 teaspoons vanilla extract, or
1 tablespoon whiskey
1 1/2 cups chopped pecans

Serves 12 to 16

The Crust: Combine the sugar, flour, milk and butter in a bowl and mix well. Pour into a 9×13-inch baking dish sprayed with nonstick cooking spray.

The Filling: Combine the corn syrup, sugar, eggs, butter, vanilla and pecans in a bowl and mix well. Spoon over the crust batter. Bake at 350 degrees for 35 to 45 minutes or until the crust is brown and the filling is very softly set. Serve warm.

Note: This dessert is very versatile. You can substitute a can of cherry, blueberry, or blackberry pie filling for the pecan filling. Or you can use the pecan filling in a prepared 9-inch deep-dish pie shell and bake as directed.

BROWNIE TORTE

1 (15-ounce) package brownie mix
2 eggs
1/2 cup water
1/2 cup chopped nuts
12 ounces whipped topping
1/4 cup packed brown sugar
2 tablespoons instant coffee granules

Serves 16

Combine the brownie mix, eggs and water in a bowl and beat until blended. Stir in the nuts. Pour into 2 greased and floured 9-inch baking pans. Bake for 35 minutes. Remove to a wire rack to cool. Combine the whipped topping, brown sugar and coffee granules in a bowl and mix well. Spread between the layers and over the top and side of the cooled brownies.

MAGIC ICE CREAM

1 teaspoon instant coffee granules
1 tablespoon hot water
1/2 cup sweetened condensed milk
4 ounces bittersweet chocolate
1/2 teaspoon vanilla extract
Pinch of salt
1 1/4 cups cold heavy whipping cream

Serves 4

Dissolve the coffee granules in the hot water in a small bowl. Combine with the sweetened condensed milk in a microwave-safe bowl. Add the chocolate and microwave for 1 minute or until the chocolate is melted, stirring every 10 seconds. Stir in the vanilla and salt and let stand until cool.

Beat the whipping cream in a bowl for 2 minutes or until soft peaks form. Whisk one-third of the whipped cream into the cooled chocolate mixture. Fold the remaining whipped cream into the chocolate mixture. Spoon into an airtight container or chocolate crumb crust and freeze for 6 hours or until firm. You may store in the freezer for up to 2 weeks.

RUSTIC BERRY TART

1 refrigerator pie pastry
Melted butter
2 1/2 cups fresh mixed berries, or
1 (16-ounce) package frozen mixed
berries, thawed and drained
3 tablespoons granulated sugar
1 tablespoon all-purpose flour
1 1/2 teaspoons orange zest
1/4 teaspoon cinnamon
Coarse sugar

Serves 6 to 8

Unfold the pastry into a deep dish pie plate, allowing the excess pastry to hang over the edge. Brush with melted butter. Combine the berries, granulated sugar, flour, orange zest and cinnamon in a bowl and stir gently. Spoon into the prepared pie plate. Drizzle with melted butter. Fold the excess pastry up and over to partially cover the filling, pleating the pastry as needed. Sprinkle the pastry with coarse sugar. Bake at 350 degrees for 1 hour or until the crust is golden brown. Serve warm with vanilla ice cream.

KEY LIME PIE

1 (14-ounce) can sweetened
condensed milk
1/4 cup egg substitute
3/4 cup Key lime juice
(approximately 12 to 15 Key limes)
1 (9-inch) baked pie shell or graham
cracker pie crust

Serves 8

Combine the condensed milk and egg substitute in a mixing bowl. Add the Key lime juice to the bowl and mix just to blend. Do not overbeat. Pour the filling into the baked pie shell. Chill overnight or until set. Top with whipped cream, if desired.

Desserts

GRANDMOTHER'S PLATE APPLE PIE

1 package refrigerator pie pastry
6 yellow Delicious apples, chopped
3 Winesap apples, chopped
1 cup sugar
2 tablespoons each all-purpose flour
and minute tapioca
3/4 teaspoon salt
1/2 teaspoon cinnamon
1/4 cup (1/2 stick) butter, sliced
3/4 cup water

Serves 8

Preheat the oven to 350 degrees. Line a 9-inch pie plate with 1 of the pie pastries. Spoon the apples into the pastry. Sprinkle with a mixture of the sugar, flour, tapioca, salt and cinnamon. Top with the butter and drizzle with the water. Cover with the remaining pastry and crimp the edges; cut slits in the top. Bake for 1 hour or until light brown.

MISS MARY'S FUDGE PIE

1/4 cup (1/2 stick) butter
1 1/2 cups sugar
3 tablespoons cocoa powder
2 eggs, beaten
1/2 cup evaporated milk
1 tablespoon Jack Daniel's®
Tennessee Whiskey
1 (9-inch) graham cracker pie crust
Sweetened whipped cream

Serves 8

Heat oven to 350 degrees. Melt butter in a saucepan over medium heat. Stir in sugar and cocoa powder. Stir in eggs, evaporated milk and Jack Daniel's®. Pour into the prepared pie crust and bake for 30 to 35 minutes or until set. Cool completely. Serve slices with a dollop of whipped cream sweetened with sugar and a little Jack Daniel's®. Sprinkle cream with a dusting of cocoa powder.

Lynne Tolley, great-grand niece of Jack Daniel and proprietress of Miss Mary Bobo's Boarding House™ in Lynchburg, Tennessee.

PUMPKIN PATCH SQUARES

2 cups self-rising flour
2 cups sugar
2 teaspoons cinnamon
4 eggs, beaten
1 cup oil
2 cups pumpkin purée
2 tablespoons Jack Daniel's®
Tennessee Whiskey
2 teaspoons vanilla
Cinnamon Cream Cheese Frosting
(below)

Serves 16

Heat oven to 350 degrees. Grease a 9×13-inch baking pan. Combine flour, sugar and cinnamon in a large mixing bowl. Stir in eggs, oil, pumpkin, Jack Daniel's® and vanilla until smooth. Pour the batter into the greased baking pan. Bake for 30 to 35 minutes or until lightly browned, firm on the top and the edges begin to pull away from the sides of the pan; cool. Spread with Cinnamon Cream Cheese Frosting.

 Lynne Tolley, great-grand niece of Jack Daniel.

CINNAMON CREAM CHEESE FROSTING

8 ounces cream cheese, softened
1/4 cup (1/2 stick) butter
1 tablespoon Jack Daniel's®
Tennessee Whiskey
2 teaspoons vanilla
1/2 teaspoon cinnamon
1 (1-pound) package
confectioners' sugar

Cream the cream cheese and butter in a large mixing bowl with an electric mixer until light and fluffy. Add the Jack Daniel's®, vanilla and cinnamon. Gradually blend in the confectioners' sugar until thick and creamy.

DECADENT TRIPLE CHOCOLATE CAKE

1 (2-layer) package devil's food
cake mix
3 eggs
1 cup water
1/4 cup vegetable oil
1/2 cup heavy whipping cream
2 tablespoons baking cocoa
2 tablespoons instant coffee granules
1 cup miniature chocolate chips
2 tablespoons heavy whipping cream
2 tablespoons instant coffee granules
2 (16-ounce) containers
vanilla frosting

Serves 12

Preheat the oven to 350 degrees. Combine the cake mix, eggs, water, oil, 1/2 cup heavy cream, the baking cocoa and 2 tablespoons coffee granules in a bowl. Beat with an electric mixer at low speed until blended. Beat at medium speed for 2 minutes. Stir in the chocolate chips. Pour into 2 greased and floured 9-inch cake pans.

Bake for 25 to 30 minutes or until a wooden pick inserted in the center comes out clean. Cool in the pans for 20 minutes. Remove to a wire rack to cool completely.

Mix 2 tablespoons heavy cream and 2 tablespoons coffee powder in a bowl. Add the vanilla frosting and stir to mix well. Spread between the layers and over the top and side of the cake.

DEVIL'S FOOD BARS

1/2 cup (1 stick) butter or margarine
1 (2-layer) package devil's food
cake mix
1 cup semisweet chocolate chips
1 cup butterscotch chips
1 cup flaked coconut
1 cup chopped pecans
1 (14-ounce) can sweetened
condensed milk

Makes 4 dozen

Preheat the oven to 350 degrees. Cut the butter into the cake mix in a large bowl with a pastry blender until crumbly. Pat over the bottom of a 10×15-inch baking pan. Sprinkle with the chocolate chips, butterscotch chips, coconut and pecans. Pour the condensed milk over the top. Bake for 20 minutes or until golden brown and puffed in the center. Cool on a wire rack. Cut into bars.

Wild Sides & Sweet Endings

Just Us
Ralph J. McDonald

International Artist of the Year
—1981, 2006

Ralph J. McDonald has a love and passion for painting beautiful wildlife and landscapes as well as children. His series, *Children's Spirit*, boasts a multitude of paintings that include young boys and girls and their hunting buddies. McDonald captures the essence of their anticipation of the hunt and their "dreams" as they are realized.

Reminisce back to childhood as these characters step out into a new world of hunting, fishing, and exploring, usually with a favorite companion nearby.

Favorites from the series include: *Dreams Come True*, *Forever Friends*, *Someday Soon*, *Serious Business*, and *Got 'em Dad*, which earned him the 2006 DU™ International Artist of the Year award.

Index

DU™ members are the best. Without our members and volunteers, wetlands conservation would severely suffer. Now I am able to enjoy terrific recipes and time-honored game cooking traditions from some of our best supporters who are making a difference for waterfowl and other game.

Jim Hulbert, Past President of Ducks Unlimited®

This page constitutes an extension of the copyright page.

Photography and Art Index

Cover and Title Page: *Fruits of Your Labor* by David Maass

Four-Color Cover background and Chapter Openers
Mike Rutherford Photography; Brad Whitfield Art Direction; Mary Ann Fowlkes, Food Styling

Endsheet: Photograph (1957) by George Purvis
   Arkansas Game and Fish Commission

Pages 6 *Beams Creek* by Dennis Minor

Pages 38 *Up the Creek* by Richard (Dick) Plasschaert

Pages 70 *Sunset Refuge* by Michael Sieve

Pages 116 *The Challenge* by Jim Hansel

Pages 138 *Crossing the River* by Bruce Miller

Pages 158 *Maybe Next Time* © Ralph J. McDonald

Pages 186 *Just Us* © Ralph J. McDonald

Pages 18, 21, 25, 114, 122, 123, 137, 140, 150, 154, 157, 166, 167 © by Eileen Clarke

Pages 16, 80,118 © by Lisa Freeman

Page 10 © by John Hoffman

Page 88 © by Lee Thomas Kjos

Pages 24, 28, 37, 44, 46, 56, 57, 61, 63, 83, 97, 99, 100, 109, 111, 128, 132, 141, 144, 153, 155, 161, 162, 165 © by Scott Leysath

Pages 12, 87, 94, 124, 127, 148, 168, 172, 175, 176, 178, 179, 180, 181, 183, 184, 185 © by Mike Rutherford Photography

Pages 6, 23, 30, 32, 38, 42, 51, 58, 69, 70, 101, 104, 116, 126, 138, 151, 158, 170, 182, 186 courtesy of Ducks Unlimited®

Executive Editor: Roger Conner
Art Direction and Book Design: Steve Newman
Editorial Director: Mary Cummings

Marketing Director: Mary Margaret Andrews
Marketing Consultant: Jeff Krinks
Project Editors: Julee Hicks, Cathy Ropp

The Hunter's Table
Wild Flavors From Duck Country

To order additional copies of this cookbook,
please visit our Web site at www.hunterstable.com or call 1-800-358-0560